0

We dedicate this book to Meghan Markle and Prince Harry, on the occasion of their wedding, 19th May 2018.

As one Anglo-American couple to another, we know only too well that you will occasionally be confused, bewildered, and to a degree, amusingly "divided" by a common language and culture.

We wish you, Good Health, Long Life, and Happiness!

Meghan Markle and Prince Harry
Photo by Mark Jones - Wikipedia

Being American

Married to a Brit©

An Amusing Guidebook for Anglo-American Couples Divided by a
Common Language and Culture

Published by MajorVision International

2018

Cover Artwork: Debra Appelwick

Contents

Preface

You would think an American Girl and British Gentleman wouldn't have a language barrier, I mean, we both come from English speaking countries, right?

Oh boy, was I wrong! Of course, when we first met I fell in love with his accent. I think most of us American ladies love the British accent. At the time, I thought that would be the only difference. We enjoy some of the best conversations I've ever experienced, and even though there are sometimes complete differences in language, we still find the amusing side of things.

Before I first visited and toured Great Britain, I didn't realize that different parts of the country have so many different regional accents. Naturally, I already knew from watching movies and TV shows in the United States that someone from Edinburgh in Scotland, has a completely different accent to someone from either Cardiff in South Wales, or Belfast in Northern Ireland.

However, when compared to the real regional accents I heard when visiting England, Scotland and Wales, some of the U.S. TV show versions of the accents weren't even close to being accurate. In fact, in one made-for-TV movie I remember well, the actor playing the Scottish Police officer from the area around Loch Ness gave a virtual guided tour of the British Isles, accent by accent, without ever getting to Scotland! I'm now looking forward to visiting both Northern and Southern Ireland very soon too.

8

Perhaps what surprised me the most was how completely different the accent was of someone from Liverpool, and someone from Manchester – cities which are only about 30 miles apart. Similarly, someone from Cornwall has a distinctively different accent from someone who is native to Newcastle, and the North East in general.

It's been a surreal, and even a strange experience at times for me as an American to listen to British people say to others "Have a nice day.", because many seem genuinely uneasy about saying this phrase, probably because they feel it may come across as being somewhat insincere.

"Awesome" is another common term that is used, or to be more precise, overused by Americans, and which the British seem uncomfortable in saying. The problem with the overuse of any word is that it soon loses any real meaning, and as such, new superlatives eventually must be found and used. The reality is, and the Brits have it right here, (so my apologies to everyone back in the States) typically when an American says that something is "awesome" it's probably because they simply don't know a more suitable and applicable substitute. We Americans need to get our act together here, because the plain truth is that everything in life which we claim is "awesome", simply isn't "awesome" in the real sense of the word.

There are just so many differences in words, sayings, and even the way you use certain words within sentences. For me at least, when I came to live in Britain it was almost like learning a whole new language. Therefore, I decided to write this book, so that it could be a useful tool for our latest addition to the Royal Family, the lovely

Meghan Markle. I've no doubt that Meghan and Prince Harry will have already experienced, and continue to experience, many of the same language and cultural gaffs that my husband and I have. They must have, because my husband and I both know that these things are inevitable.

In addition, I sincerely hope that this book will be useful for all Anglo-American couples, or anyone else for that matter, who may be traveling to the United Kingdom and wants to learn more about the language and cultural differences waiting for them when they arrive. We hope that you find this book amusing, entertaining and generally helpful. We're just pleased to be able to share some of our real-life adventure stories with you, and sincerely wish you every happiness and success in life!

Chapter 1: The Cornwall Connection

It all started for me in a place called North Pole, Alaska, and yes, there really is a town in Alaska called North Pole. In 1981 my parents broke the bad news to my twin sister and I that my Father had lost his job at the Glendenning Trucking Company, because they had closed their doors and gone out of business.

This could have either been a huge disaster for us, or a golden opportunity, and thankfully it was the latter thanks to my Father's positive approach to life. So, just as in the great John Wayne movie, and yes, my parents were great fans of "The Duke", we packed up our home and headed "North to Alaska" and an entirely new way of l fe. The entire family were right behind him, and we supported him all the way.

The move to Alaska was huge, because it was over 3,000 miles from the town where I'd been born, which was Duluth, in Northern Minnesota. Perfectly situated on Lake Superior, Duluth played a significant part the birth of Minnesota as a State. It quickly grew in prominence due to the rich iron ore fields it sits on, and because it was the gateway port which shipped all the grain that was grown on the great American prairies out to Europe, and the rest of the world.

The plan was that when we moved to Alaska my Father, William Wuorio, or "Minnesota Bill" as he quickly became known, could follow his dream and become an Ice Road Trucker, just like those portrayed in the modern TV series. It had been his dream job for a long time, and he eventually decided to take the plunge when the opportunity had been forced upon him due to sudden unemployment.

When we first moved to Alaska, my Father initially helped to support us by selling trucks with his brother Pete. This business very soon helped to provide the extra cash needed so that my Father could buy his own truck to haul commercial goods on the world-famous James Dalton Hwy, AKA, "The Haul Road".

Life in Alaska was very different to life in Minnesota in many ways. For example, I remember simply looking out of our kitchen window one day, only to come face to face with a huge moose staring back at me. Amazingly, it was almost expressing a "moose smile" if they do such a thing. The Northern Lights were simply incredible, and then the almost 24 hours of constant daylight in summer, and almost perpetual darkness in winter, both took a lot of getting used to. Then there's the cold. Minnesota is very cold in winter, but by Alaskan standards the worst Minnesotan winter is almost like the best of weather in Alaska. I even remember on my prom night that, with wind chill, it was over 60 degrees Fahrenheit below zero. In fact, it was so cold that I heard about someone from my school who slammed their car door closed, only to have it literally fall right off because it had become brittle due to extreme cold metal fatigue!

Another fun little fact about our family is that we are now officially named as being "Pioneers" of Alaska, along with several other folks. There is a monument located in downtown Fairbanks, Alaska, at Golden Heart Plaza with a statue from Malcolm Alexander's "Unknown

First Family" and it has our names engraved on a plaque surrounding it, proudly listed as pioneers of the State.

We had been living in Alaska for a couple of years when one day, a random traveling salesman came knocking on our door. Such salesmen weren't uncommon, but this time it was different. My mother was never the type to buy anything from a random door-to-door salesman, so you can imagine my surprise when we got home from school and she proudly showed us what she had purchased that day. She said that the salesman was selling framed pictures, and he had quite a selection to choose from. After chatting and browsing a while, my mother eventually bought a couple of foil framed prints of a beautiful tiny fishing village. I remember her saying that even though the salesman had lots of pictures for sale, for some reason she kept being drawn back to this picture, and its companion. As soon as I saw them, I fell in love with both of those pictures too.

Naturally, having never experienced anywhere like the places portrayed in the images in those pictures, I simply assumed that the depictions were some sort of fantasy fishing village that were perhaps at best, loosely based on somewhere real.   For the entire time we lived in Alaska, my parents always had both prints proudly displayed on the walls of our home.

I have no idea why, but I found these pictures simply fascinating, compelling in fact. Such was the strength of my attraction to them, that I was almost paranormally drawn to them. I would gaze at them for

POLPERRO, CORNWALL, ENGLAND - PHOTO BY HELEN RENÉE WUORIO 2016

hours on end while I was lounging around relaxing on the sofa after school, often dreaming about walking through the beautiful village streets portrayed in those pictures. I'd envision every step I'd take, the feel of the uneven cobbled streets under my feet, and every sight I'd experience when I paused to look over the harbour wall. The smell of the fresh ocean breeze, and the newly budding flowers in the window boxes of the perfect cottages I'd walk past in my

15

dreams. This was the special place of my teenage years, in fact it was my secret place. It was the place of my dreams, and I'd retreat there in my mind whenever life at high school became too much for me as a teenager growing up into a young woman.

Many years later when my Father decided to semi-retire, and by that time, the whole family was living back in our native Minnesota. His semi-retirement would allow him to spend all the time he wanted fishing, and generally hanging around in a boat on one of the State's reputed 10,000 lakes.

However, his retirement also meant down-sizing their home to a new one near the Twin Cities, and then to an even smaller home in Northern Minnesota on Lake Mille Lacs. A smaller home naturally meant that there was going to be less room to hang all their pictures on the walls, and when the crunch-time came my Mom wasn't sure what to do with the foil pictures of the fantasy fishing villages I loved so much. I didn't waste a second, and immediately asked if I could have them for my own home, and I was thrilled that she said yes!

Fast-forward to 2015. By this time, I was happily divorced, and living "the dream" of a country girl in the big city of Minneapolis, Minnesota. More importantly, and by this time I was on a second date with a handsome gentleman from Manchester, England, Brian Sterling-Vete. After our first date we already knew that we were very attracted to each other, and we had many things in common, so we weren't going to be short of conversation.

At the time, I was training to compete in my first Bikini Fitness Bodybuilding Contest, and since I'd learned that Brian was a highly acclaimed exercise science expert, I was going to pick his brains about exercise and nutrition. When he dropped me back at home that evening, I invited him inside to discuss the meal plan I was on, and the myriad of vitamins and supplements I was taking. While I was explaining my supplement regimen, I noticed that Brian had become distracted, and had become transfixed by the foil prints on the wall of my "fantasy" fishing village.

I asked him if anything was wrong. He then turned to me with a look of utter amazement on his face, and asked, "Why do you have my fishing village on your wall?" I was stunned. He then proceeded to tell me that this was the first place his Mother had taken him on holiday as a small child, and the last place he had taken his Mother on holiday before she passed away. It was his parents all-time favourite place, and it was his too. The picture he was staring at, a place that for years I had believed only existed

HELEN AND BRIAN STANDING ON THE HARBOUR WALL IN POLPERRO, CORNWALL, ENGLAND 2017

in fantasy, in the minds-eye of the artist, was apparent y real. It was Polperro, in Cornwall, England.

I was completely shocked, and Immediately locked at him and said "Well if that isn't a sign! You might as well put a ring on it now!" while semi-jokingly holding my left hand up, with my wedding ring finger extended. He immediately said "YES!" and we both laughed.

HELEN AND BRIAN JUST MARRIED 2016
WITH OUR ASTON MARTIN DB10 JAMES BOND SKYFALL EDITION

The rest as the saying goes, is history. We're now happily married, and quite naturally we visited Polperro for our honeymoon. In fact, we've been on holiday to Polperro multiple times already. Ah, that's the first lesson I learned, because what the British call a "Holiday", we call a "Vacation". I was learning something already. When I first used the term vacation to my new husband, he said, "Vacate where? If you mean that you're vacating a place or premises then it might make more sense, but we're not, because we're only going to take a break from working darling, so we're actually going on a holiday."

If you ever get the chance to visit the UK, and, Cornwall, then visiting Polperro is an absolute must. It is a truly magical place!

MEVAGISSEY, CORNWALL, ENGLAND FOIL PRINT

The sister print to this beautiful place puzzled us for quite a while. We knew that it must be another tiny fishing village in England, and Brian thought it looked familiar but couldn't quite place it. On our last holiday to Polperro, we decided to go out and explore some of the other little Cornish villages nearby. We were on our way to St. Mawes when I noticed an old large-scale road map in one of the map pockets on the cart seat. Even though we hardly ever use a physical map these days thanks to satellite navigation, I had the urge to open it up and see what the most scenic route to take might be.

Suddenly, for some reason the word "Mevagissey" metaphorically popped right off the page at me. I thought that was odd because I had never heard of that place before. I asked Brian if he had heard of it. He remembered visiting there with his parents when he was a very young child, but since it was so long ago he couldn't remember any details about the village except that it was a nice place. I then decided to search for "Mevagissey" on my cell phone browser, and as soon as I saw a photo of it I knew that we simply had to visit.

I clearly remember that I screamed aloud to Brian, "WE HAVE TO GO HERE TODAY!" He just rolled his eyes in confusion and continued driving. I then said to him, "This is it! This was the other picture on my wall!" We'd found it, I was trembling with joy and excitement. We had finally solved the puzzle of the other foil print.

MEVAGISSEY, CORNWALL, ENGLAND PHOTO BY HELEN WUORIO

We immediately changed our plans, so I re-routed the satellite navigation to head to Mevagissey, and it was even prettier than I could have ever imagined. The narrow cobblestone streets, the tiny fishing boats in the harbour and the signature stone wall that I had imagined walking in front of was right there across the harbour.

I'd done it all now! I'd already walked the streets of Polperro, which are so tiny you can hardly drive a small car down, and I'd now lived my dream of walking the streets of my other "fantasy" fishing village, Mevagissey. I'd literally walked right "into" the old foil pictures I'd treasured since my early teenage years.

Chapter 2: Loo, Restroom, and W.C.

On our first trip to Manchester, since there was no direct flight, we decided to fly into the U.K. via London and then drive North by car to Manchester so he could show me some of the country along the way. When we stopped at a motorway service area on the M40 near Oxford, I was confused because I couldn't see any signs indicating where the "restrooms" were, or indeed if there were any at all.

Instead, I saw several signs saying W.C. "What the heck? Why does it say W.C.? What does that mean?", I ask.

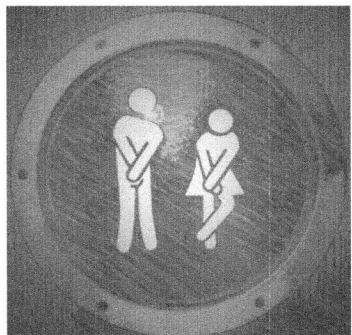

Brian then proceeds to explain to me that W.C. is an abbreviation for "Water Closet" which was the original name for a flush toilet. This was also when I learned that the Brits don't call it a restroom, and that I'd never see a sign for one when in the U.K. Instead I needed to lookout for signs saying W.C., or Toilets, or even Loo.

Brian then also asked me why Americans call it a restroom because no one ever uses one to genuinely take a rest in. I stopped to think about this for a moment and I had to admit that he was right. The more I thought about it, the more that the term "Restroom" makes no sense, especially when one considers what those places are really used for. Why don't we Americans simply call it what it is, a toilet? I believe it's because Americans think it is a politer way to say toilet. For some reason, we think we are being more discreet by saying restroom or bathroom.

After I'd visited the "loo", I walked out laughing so much that my husband, who was waiting for me outside, asked me what was wrong. I then explained that even though I expected to find some cultural differences in the U.K., I was genuinely surprised that they really call the restroom "the loo" and now even more surprised to learn that they even run a national competition to find the best

loo! Apparently, I'd had the enormous good fortune to not simply visit just any old loo, I'd paid a visit to the winner of the 2016 "Loo of the Year" contest!

American tourists who are visiting the U.K., beware! I have also noticed you should never simply ask for a bathroom. This is because in many private homes, the bathrooms often only have the bathtub and sink in the room, and no toilet. Occasionally even the sink is not in the same room as the toilet. When you do finally find the sink, you will probably notice that the hot and cold-water taps are separate, and not a single mixer tap, or faucet as we would call it in the United States. I am not saying this is the way of things in all homes in Britain, but if they have mixer taps, then it would most likely be in a newer home, or an older one which has been re-fitted. So, Americans, please remember that if you are urgently needing to "go", then be sure to ask for either the toilet or the loo to save you time, and possible embarrassment.

One of the phrases related to this function that I heard from my British girlfriend is, "I'm going to spend a penny.", which I had never heard before. This phrase comes from the time when you needed to pay a penny, usually in a doorway fitted payment slot, to use a public toilet. They do still have them in several places around the U.K., but they cost a lot more than a penny these days. Therefore, I'd strongly advise visitors to the U.K. to plan ahead, and source some British coins to prevent you finding yourself needing to urgently use a public loo, but don't have the local currency to help you in your quest.

Whilst on the subject of "going", a male British friend always says, "I'm going to squeeze the lemon." While his wife, sometimes says, "I'm going to squeeze the peach." I think that both terms are self-explanatory once

you stop and think about them for a moment. I then invented my own term, which has since caused more than a few laughs at social events. I proudly once announced at a Christmas party with a few British friends that, "I'm going to squeeze a penny!" They all paused in silence for a moment, before breaking out into fits of hysterical laugher at my complete butchery of both phrases. As the words came out of my mouth, I instinctively knew that I had said it all wrong. No matter, perhaps I will get it right eventually, or not...

Another language difference in relation to bathrooms and sinks, is in the faucet as we Americans call them, or taps, as the Brits call them. In the U.K. the term tap almost always refers to an everyday type of supply valve fitted to control the water supply to bathtubs and sinks. Technically, a tap is also known as a spigot, or a faucet. More commonly, the term spigot refers to a tap used by professionals such as plumbers which are usually located outdoors. Whereas a silcock refers to a cock or stopcock that penetrates the foundation of a building. In the United States, a tap generally refers to a beer tap. Hence the common term, tap house.

Petrol/Gas Stations and Restrooms/Loo. This is a warning to all of us Americans who are spoiled by the availability of having a restroom, AKA loo/toilet etc., in almost every gas/petrol station on every street corner. This does NOT exist in Britain.

If you visit a petrol station here, then there's almost never going to be any "facility" for you to use, no matter how desperate you are. You've been warned! The best thing to do is to plan you journey around your needs, unless you're a big fan of wearing those adult diapers/nappies!

Chapter 3: Who Invented this Language?

English takes its name from the Anglia peninsula in the North Sea, and there is still an area called East Anglia in Britain today. It is now a fusion of Frisian, German, Norse, Latin and French. Perhaps this is the reason why it can be so perplexing at times.

The English language obviously wasn't "invented" as such, rather it formed over a period of more than 1,400 years of fusion, invasion, conquest, and integration with other people from many other countries. Modern English began roughly in the late 1500's, and then spread rapidly thanks to the invention of the printing press, and the King James version of the Bible. Basically, English is a West Germanic language, and modern English was spoken from roughly mediaeval times onwards.

This is the point in time onwards when the English, would eventually become the British through the union with Scotland, Wales and Ireland. As the British Empire, spread and grew, modern English spread and grew globally with it from the 17th century onwards. At its height, the British Empire was the largest empire in history, and for over a century Britain ruled over 412 million people, or ¼ of the population of the world at the time. It also covered over ¼ of the world's landmass. This is why, no matter if you like it or not, English has now become the international language of the entire planet.

Thinking about how the English language has been changed since it first came to the North American continent with the settlers from 1620 onwards, surprised me considerably. I soon found myself shocked at how little I'd been taught, or possibly just don't remember being taught, anything of substance at school about how it all began for the United States as a nation.

I'd hazard a guess that most of my fellow Americans have absolutely no idea of the real story behind how the country first came to be settled. It's almost like they were only taught a sanitised, brief media-friendly overview version at school. Most have never even heard about Robert Browne of the Lilford Estate, in Northamptonshire, England, and how he was the key figure instrumental in teaching the Mayflower settlers their values and religion.

I was tempted to use the word "pilgrim" in that last sentence, but thanks to my new knowledge, that would have been incorrect. This is because the word "pilgrim" wasn't used when referring to the Mayflower settlers until about 1820, almost 200 years after Plymouth Colony was first founded. I learned that the settlers weren't even just the friends and strangers, and the majority were followers of Robert Browne, and were therefore called the Brownist Emigration.

Thanks to my husband's work in producing a major TV documentary about all of this in 2013, I've now visited Lilford Hall and the Lilford Estate where Robert Browne lived. Interestingly, several other people from the Lilford Estate were also instrumental in the formation of the United States as a nation. One ultra-significant person was

27

the mother of George Washington, our first President, and others were the family who would eventually produce President Quincy Adams. What would have happened to the American Colonies without George Washington being born? Who knows...

It was during my visit to the Lilford Estate when the subject arose about what kind of English dialect the original settlers would have had. The Squire of the estate, Nathan, had a good suggestion about this. He had worked closely with the full-time resident historian who had been employed for the TV documentary. It was suggested that the was most likely accent of the original Mayflower settlers would have sounded something like a strong Cornish, or West Country accent of today.

It's also a fact that the original settlers weren't from the upper echelons of English society, instead, they were dissidents opposed to Queen Elizabeth the 1st and the Church of England at the time. Therefore, their use of the English language would have been somewhat limited and include many slang words of the time. Over time, as the American colonies became more important economically, the better educated settlers arrived, along with their "proper" use of the English language to add to the mix.

I also learned that at the time of the revolution, the use of the letter "R" was typically fully pronounced within words used by those with higher social status.

Over time, due to isolation from the mother-country, and through settlers arriving from many other countries in Europe, the English language eventually changed to become the American version of English we speak today. Let's not forget that Native Americans also added new words to the evolving language to describe animals which were only native to North America.

With the revolutionary war over, the new "Americans" decided to deliberately change words in the English language thanks to Mr Webster, the creator of Webster's dictionary. In 1789 Noah Webster wrote "Dissertations on the English Language", and in it he said, "As an independent nation, our honor requires us to have a system of our own, in language as well as government."

It seems that after the revolution we Americans deliberately changed many words just for the sake of change, and to be different to the country they had just broken away from. Many of those changes remain to this day, but even at the time many people thought that Webster was going way too far in trying to change words in his dictionaries. Therefore, many of the additional deliberate changes he wanted to make were quashed.

Today, American English is not really that different to original English. However, it's different enough for me to be deliberately annoying to my husband when we're having our fun conversations about language and spelling.

The day after we had returned from our honeymoon I woke to find a funny message from our son, who is in the U.S. Military and had been temporarily stationed in Britain for the first time. The message that I woke up to in my inbox simply said, "Carriageway, Boot, Bonnet, Lorrie, Pelican Crossing? Who made up this language?!" He obviously said this jokingly, and the rest of the message was about how he and his companions were thoroughly enjoying their first visit to Britain.

I had to chuckle to myself about it though, because when I first visited Britain I had noticed the very same things that he was now noticing. However, the English "invented" the English language, so in one way, they should know how to speak and pronounce classical English. I like to tease my husband about this, and then add that, "Yes, your people may have invented the language, but we Americans perfected it!" When I say this, he just shakes his head, rolls his eyes, and smiles...

Chapter 4: Anglo-American Humour

British and American humour (or 'humor' if you're American) are two very different things, and for the most part they somehow manage to interconnect. However, on occasion there are some aspects of both British and

American humour that will leave the other party staring blankly and open-mouthed wondering what all the fuss and laughter was about.

Generally, British humour finds its roots in the absurdity of the class system, the monotonous stability of traditional British life, sexual taboos, and every-day life in general; all wrapped up with generous helpings of good old innuendo. Whereas American humour finds its roots in observation of cultural differences, with more slapstick and physical comedy than British humour.

Perhaps the biggest shock in respect of trying to understand British humour was when I was first introduced to the "Carry On" series of 31 classic comedy motion pictures made between 1958–92. I'd already experienced the heavy and harmless innuendo style of humour at times before even seeing one of the "Carry On" movies, but I'd absolutely no idea that it was so deeply ingrained at the heart of British culture. My husband had told me in advance about the British comic tradition of the music hall, and the bawdy seaside postcards which became commonplace as a result, and which still exist today.

We had watched all the "Carry On" movies through the first Christmas and New Year's season I spent in Britain, and they eventually grew on me. I then found out in the media that Her Majesty Queen Elizabeth II had been ill over the Christmas season, and apparently, she had watched the same "Carry On" movies that we had while she was recovering. So, in a way I was in the company of Royalty!

American humour tends to be generally more open, without the British tendencies towards exaggerated satirical observation of the social system. It's much more observation oriented, highlighting the differences and ridiculousness of certain aspects of American culture and social discourse. American humour is much more linear in nature, and unlike the British, we Americans love and support ambition because we genuinely believe that we can do almost anything. Whereas the British tend to love and support the underdog and losers, because they have been brought up to believe they should be happy with their lot in life. Unsurprisingly then, British humour generally has a strong theme of self-deprecation and sarcasm woven into it, usually with a straight-faced comedic delivery of the punchline.

The British would typically use the word "marvellous" or "fabulous" instead of "awesome", but thinking about it in reverse, I don't think that many Americans would feel comfortable and sincere if they said, "marvellous" or "fabulous" as much as they say "awesome". I am one-hundred percent guilty of this myself, and I'm now trying to break the habit by deliberately limiting any overuse of the word "awesome".

Other classic hallmarks of British humour are based around the class system, and the "I'm terribly sorry" culture they seem to be brought up with. The perfect way to observe these unique British cultural elements in action, and several others too, is by watching the BBC comedy masterpiece of Fawlty Towers. John Cleese perfectly portrays the typical product of the British class system as he bows, scrapes, and doffs his cap to anyone he considers to be even slightly higher on the social scale then he is. John Cleese, as hotel owner Basil Fawlty, is completely in awe of anyone who is a doctor, or in any kind of professional occupation, while at the same time treating everyone else with complete disdain. John Cleese co-wrote it with his American-born wife Connie Booth, and in my opinion, they nailed it completely. They totally encapsulated the essence of British humour in only 12 TV episodes, and at the same time took a lovely sideswipe at Americans, and American humour when an Anglo-American couple stayed at the hotel in an episode called "Waldorf Salad".

Our close friend Jane Hughes was once visiting us in Minnesota, and she was telling us how her daughter teases her about being "high-maintenance", even though she doesn't believe she is. While we were on the 45-minute drive home from the airport she then complains, "It's too hot, can you open the window?" So, we open a window, and then within a few minutes you hear her chirp from the backseat, "It's too windy, can you just turn the air conditioning on instead?" We oblige and turn the AC on.

Within a few minutes of that she then says, "I'm too cold, can you shut the air conditioning off?" My husband and I just glance at each other knowingly and exclaim together, "Miss high-maintenance! We think your daughter is right!". Then we then all broke out into hysterical laughter.

My husband then began calling her "Rosewood, Mahogany, Teak?" I had no idea what that meant, so he explained that it's taken from an episode of the brilliantly scripted "Fawlty Towers" TV show, the episode "The Kipper and the Corpse". In that episode, a guest who is staying at the hotel is being offered the breakfast in bed service by the hotel

JANE, HELEN AND BRIAN

owner's wife. The guest accepts, and as he's walking upstairs the hotel owner played by the fantastic John Cleese sarcastically mumbles, "Rosewood, Mahogany, Teak?" in relation to what kind of wood the guest would prefer his breakfast tray to be made from. Hence why we associate the phrase with meaning, high maintenance. If you have never seen it, then I highly recommend that you watch all 12 amazing episodes.

Naturally, no offence was meant, or taken, so we all had a good laugh about it, and now whenever one of us is acting in even a slightly high-maintenance way, all we have to say to stop it is, "Rosewood, Mahogany, Teak?"

Jane is one of our many close friends who makes a 50/50 Anglo-American lifestyle work in practice. She is originally from Cheshire, England, but has lived 50% of each year in Florida for the last 15 years.

Chapter 5: Cuppa Tea Please

Tea is a British institution, it's that simple. There is the traditional English tea, herbal tea, green tea, cream

tea's and many more types of tea. In fact, when you visit Britain, you will have almost endless options for tea. The first time we visited the home of our friends Stuart and Sharon Hurst, I was asked if I would like a "cuppa tea?" I said sure, Sharon then asks me if I would like regular milk, soy, or almond milk in it.

Initially, such a suggestion seemed crazy to me. Why would you put milk in your tea? Surprisingly to many, it's common behaviour in England. If you have tea in England in a tea shop, then you'll often

notice people adding milk to their tea. To my surprise, it

was quite delicious, and it's even better when you add a biscuit (cookie) to go with it.

You'll frequently see signs advertising, "Cream Tea" on offer throughout Devon and Cornwall. A cream tea is an afternoon English Tea, traditionally served with a scone, clotted cream and jam. Clotted cream is made from milk and cooked in a way so that when it cools the cream rises and "clots" at the top. Since I don't consume dairy products I have never tried this, and it looks more like a kind of butter to me, but I cannot tell you what the taste is like. However, I'm assured that it's delicious.

One thing I was very surprised about is the lack of good coffee in the UK. Coming from Minnesota I have my favourite which is Caribou Coffee, and then my next favourite brand which is Starbucks. If I make coffee at home when I'm in the United States, I also like to complete the experience by adding a touch of almond milk vanilla creamer.

Since I like my coffee strong, when I am out shopping or travelling, I'll typically order an Americano. However, the first time I ordered an Americano in Britain I took one sip and almost spat it out. It tasted like water! I asked quite loudly, "What on earth is this?" I then found out that an Americano coffee in England is nothing more than a plain black coffee. After being used to drinking a quad-shot Americano in Minnesota, the British attempt was simply terrible.

However, I'd learned a valuable lesson. My fellow Americans, when you're ordering an Americano coffee when visiting Britain, you'll need to ask for a shot of espresso with your Americano. Be careful though, because not all coffee shops serve good tasting coffee, not even some national chain brands. I have had to endure some awful coffee, and even though I've spent hours trying different coffee shops and brands, it's still a daily struggle.

During my first shopping expedition at the local Sainsburys supermarket in Manchester, I was very surprised

to find that the only coffee creamer that s commonly sold in Britain is powdered creamer. "What?! Are you serious?!", are my immediate thoughts. It's already challenging enough for me because I don't consume any dairy products, so whatever we buy must either be almond, soy, or coconut. They have a great selection of these things in America, but to date, I've not found any sort of selection of good coffee creamers in Britain.

If you ever visit a Target store in Minnesota, then you will know precisely what I am talking about. In my local Target store in Minneapolis, we have a whole aisle dedicated to different types of coffee creamer! I finally resorted to making my own creamer by combining soya cream together with a type of flavouring for coffee. Since we now have almond milk at our local Sainsbury's supermarket, my next experiment will be mixing that with other flavourings.

Eventually, I found a great coffee and snack shop on the high street in most British cities, it's called Pret a Manger. I highly recommended them for their good value, their healthy choices, and their tasty food and drink. I can especially recommend their "Coconut Flat White" coffee. Of course, we do have the Starbucks brand in Britain, and if you can find one of them then you'll get a good standard of real American-style coffee.

I guess that all this talk about my picky-ness of coffee brands and creamer choices makes me sound a little high-maintenance in this respect, but I'm honestly not. I prefer to think that I'm only being a slightly "Rosewood, Mahogany, Teak" as my husband would say. Since we travel transatlantic on a regular basis, I now bring plenty of my favourite Caribou brand of coffee grounds with me. The problem is that apparently criminals also use coffee grounds

41

as a means of smuggling contraband, so I've no idea what the customs officers will make about the large quantities of coffee grounds in my luggage every time we fly!

In certain parts of Britain, mostly in the North, you'll occasionally hear people refer to tea, as a mealtime, and this is also known as high tea. Referring to a meal as "tea", was traditionally a working-class term, however, in more recent years this use seems to have changed and shifted into more common use with all classes. When people use this term now, it's typically said with a degree of sarcasm, such as, "Shall we have our tea then?"

One evening we were saying good-bye to our friend Jane after she made us a lovely meal, when Brian says to her, "Thank you for the tea." I then chirp-in and say, "Honey, you forgot to thank her for the dinner too." They both just grinned at each other and laughed as they reminded me that "tea" can also mean a meal.

This is where it can all become a little confusing. In certain working-class parts of the North of Britain, South Wales, Scotland, and both Northern and Southern Ireland, it's not uncommon to hear lunch, referred to as dinner. Fortunately for visitors to Britain, this practice is much less common than it was only 30 or 40 years ago.

High tea typically consists of a cup of tea, a hot dish, together with cakes and bread, butter and jam. Sometimes, people may add a savoury touch and include some cold cuts of meat into the mix. The term "high tea" first entered use around 1825, and probably because "high tea" is taken on a high dining table. As if all of this isn't confusing enough, I also found out that there is something called a low tea. This is more of a light snack which was typically served on a low type of table, which we would commonly call a coffee table in North America.

Today, a formal afternoon tea is sort of a special occasion, often taken in a hotel. In such places, food is often served on a multi-tiered stand, and they occasionally serve sandwiches. However, it's mostly served with scones, butter, clotted cream and jam. My favourite type of high tea treat in a hotel is when the experience is made even more special with the addition of a glass of either Champagne or Prosecco!

No section would be complete in describing the British and their unusual tea rituals without describing the great British tea break. This isn't a mealtime as such, instead, it's more of an opportunity to stop work for a while and relax with a cup of tea for about 10 to 15 minutes. Typically, a tea break will be taken during the mid-morning, and mid-afternoon. If the morning tea break is taken at, or around, 11am, then this could also be referred to as elevenses. Confused? Just imagine how confused I was when I faced all this full-on when I first visited Britain for our honeymoon!

I should also mention that when you're at work, and if you leave your desk to fetch either tea or coffee for yourself without offering to bring some for your colleagues, then it's considered rude. So, you've been warned!

Oh yes, the Brits don't use the American term, "co-worker", and instead, they will typically say, "colleague".

Chapter 6: Brits and Show Tunes

It is my belief that all British people break out into song when the urge arises. Well, this probably isn't always the case, it just happens to be that all my husband and his friends seem to do that.

We were once travelling in Britain with our American friend, Danny Lopez, who is Johnny Depp's official double, and his British fiancé, Claire Renvoize, who just happens to be Kylie Minogue's double. I'm sure that you can imagine some of  the funny encounters we have when the people we meet think that they're the real celebrities! These stories could fill an entire book, and we hope they will write one.

On one occasion, we had enjoyed a great day traveling to visit both Whitby and York, and we stopped to relax over a "nice cuppa tea" in a little tea shop in York. As it happened, the walls of the shop had been covered with sheet music covers from some of the world's best musical shows. Suddenly, my husband Brian, and Claire both break-out into a selection

of songs from those shows. Danny and I were literally dumbstruck, and just looked at each other with blank faces. As they looked at the different song sheets on the walls, they'd just carry on singing song after song while we waited for our tea to arrive. I was even more surprised to learn that they both knew every word, and both were singing to their hearts content.

My husband doesn't support me in my belief about Brits and show tunes. However, fast forward to a Christmas party we were attending in Maple Grove, Minnesota. We have a group of friends in Minnesota, and four of the 8 of people who comprise our merry little group are British. We were playing board games after a great meal, and whenever a reference to a song came along, guess what? Every British person in the room started singing. It's like they have a sixth sense, and they all start at the same time, and even more amazingly, they're generally all singing in tune. My husband had no defence for this overwhelming evidence, and he now agrees that maybe the phenomena is real. Perhaps British people do tend to break out in to Broadway show tunes at every opportunity.

Theatre. In the United States we spell it with an "er" and not "re" at the end, making it "theater" to us Americans, and this will be the same with many other words as well. One day, Brian asked me to search online the directions to Manchester's Trafford Centre, so, I immediately typed into my phone, "Trafford Center". My web browser couldn't find it anywhere. it was then that I finally realized I was spelling "center" the American way, with the "er" at the end, and not the British way. As soon as I typed it the British way, I instantly found the directions we needed. You will notice other words like, flavour, colour, and honour all have a "u" in it as well. At first you might think that I spelled these words incorrectly, but this is the British way of spelling them. I'm also sure that no matter how many times this book gets proof-read, that we'll still find an occasional missed mix of Anglo-American spellings here and there.

Pantomime. When we arrived to spend Christmas in Manchester in 2016, Brian was very excited to take me to a Pantomime. I was unimpressed at the prospect because I was thinking about a performance by people who paint their face white and then mime the actions. I wondered how they can make an entire show out of such a thing? I was completely wrong in that assumption.

A Pantomime, or all the Brits call it a "Panto", is a type of musical comedy stage production suitable for adults and children of all ages. It was originally developed in England, and Panto is now performed throughout Britain typically during the Christmas and New Year season. Panto usually includes songs, gags, slapstick comedy, and dancing combined into a story which is loosely based on a well-known fairy tale, fable or folk tale such as Dick Whittington, or Sleeping Beauty. In Panto, the Dame is always played by a man, the lead male character, such as Prince Charming, is usually played by a girl. Confused yet? I certainly was...

It's a participatory form of theatre, so be warned. As a member of the audience you'll be expected to sing along during certain parts of the show, and to shout out certain phrases loudly to the performers. I found myself really enjoying that part of the show, especially during the traditional "ghost gag" scene where the performers find themselves in a haunted house.

During this scene you'll be expected to shout out things like, "It's behind you!", when the supposed ghost is creeping up on the performers. This gag typically involves each of the performers being scared from the stage one-by-one by the ghost. However, when the ghost then sees the man dressed as the dame face-to-face, the ghost is then scared and runs off the stage. The last line usually goes to the dame with something like, "Charming!".

I especially love that during intermission they bring groups of children onto the stage from the audience to perform a song. The children really love it and it's a great family event. I went to see both "Dick Whittington" and "Aladdin". They were both spectacular. If you haven't already seen a Pantomime, I then highly recommend that you see one.

Chapter 7: The Brits Know Their History

Bonfire Night. I'm embarrassed to admit that history wasn't a strong subject of mine at school. I just never really cared for it, or perhaps it was because I had teachers that were so monotonous and uninspiring that all I wanted to do was to fall asleep during their classes. At times when chatting with my husband, I also sometimes wonder if we were taught even a remotely similar version of world history.

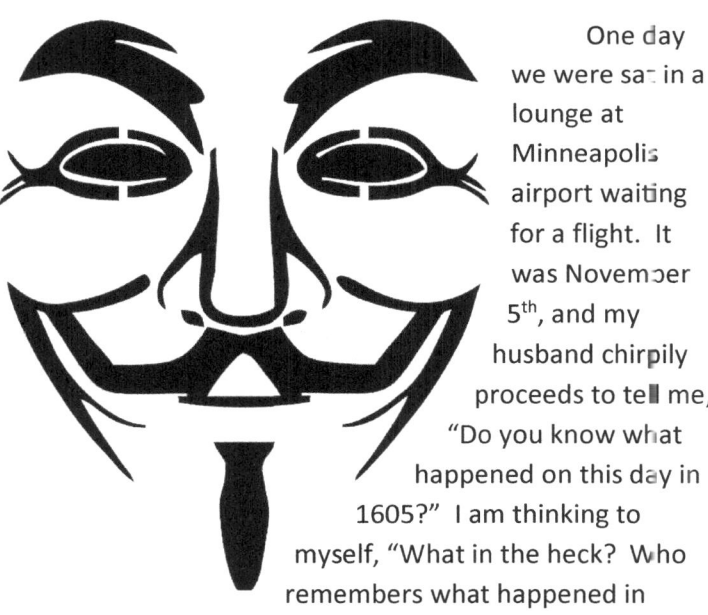

One day we were sat in a lounge at Minneapolis airport waiting for a flight. It was November 5th, and my husband chirpily proceeds to tell me, "Do you know what happened on this day in 1605?" I am thinking to myself, "What in the heck? Who remembers what happened in 1605, especially this early in the morning? You have got to be kidding me." Apparently, my husband is one of those people who does remember, and he then proceeds to tell me exuberantly. "Today is Guy Fawkes day! Which is a so known as Bonfire night!"

History teaches us that Guy Fawkes was perhaps the world's first modern terrorist. He was a member of the Gunpowder Plot and was arrested while guarding the explosives that his group of terrorists had placed  underneath the House of Lords in London. Since that time, the people of Britain light bonfires all over the country every November the 5th to celebrate the defeat of this early form of terrorism.

After my husband had told me the entire story of Guy Fawkes and the tradition of Bonfire night, I turn to him and said "Honey, if I don't find something useful every day I won't use it, and don't remember it. It's a wonder I remember I'm married to you every day!" Now this may sound mean and cutting, but it's not, because we love to joke with each other a lot. Rarely do I make him speechless, however, this was one of the times that I did. He just burst out in to fits of uncontrollable laughter, and as always, immediately saw the funny side of my great comeback line.

In England Bonfire night is a big deal, everyone has Bonfire celebrations as well as fireworks displays. In fact, there are probably more firework used every year on that night than there are during the 4th of July celebrations in the

United States. I'm very excited to experience my first Bonfire night this fall since I'm now living in Britain.

There are multiple versions of the famous "The Fifth of November" poem, here is one below I found from the website http://www.potw.org

The Fifth of November - English Folk Verse (c. 1870)

Remember, Remember!
The fifth of November,
The Gunpowder Treason and plot;
I know of no reason
Why the Gunpowder treason
Should ever be forgot!
Guy Fawkes and his companions
Did the scheme contrive,
To blow the King and Parliament
All up alive!
Threescore barrels, laid below,
To prove old England's overthrow.
But, by God's providence, him they catch,
With a dark lantern, lighting a match!
A stick and take
For King James' sake!
If you won't give me one,
I'll take two,
The better for me,

And the worse for you.
A rope, a rope, to hang the Pope,
A penn'orth of cheese to choke him,
A pint of beer to wash it down,
And a jolly good fire to burn him.
Holloa, boys! Make the bells ring!
Holloa, boys! God save the King!
Hip, hip, hooor-r-r-ray!

British People and Inventions that Helped Shape History.

The British have a long and prestigious legacy of invention and innovation. In fact, not many Americans will even realise that the Global Industrial Revolution began in Britain from about 1760 onwards. Since that time, Britain, and Manchester in particular, has been at the forefront of much of the science and engineering that has helped to shape our modern world as we know it today.

Rolls Royce. I will never forget my first tour of Manchester with my husband during our honeymoon, and the first place he took me to, which was The Midland Hotel. Did you know that Manchester is where the world-famous luxury car company Rolls Royce was formed? I didn't until I visited there. It was at Midland Hotel in Manchester centre where Charles Rolls who was a car salesman, met Henry Royce who was an  Engineer. The Midland Hotel is the location where they agreed to go into business together, and the rest is history.

The First Railway Train Station. The world's first inter-city passenger railway was built in 1830. It connected the cities of Manchester and Liverpool together, and the railway station on Liverpool Road in Manchester is now the world's oldest

remaining railway station. It's part of a large living museum called the Museum of Science and Industry, and the best part of all, is that it's free to enter.

William Worrall Mayo. William Mayo was born in Salford, which is part of Greater Manchester. He is better known for his private practice in Rochester, Minnesota. Fast-forward in time, and this Manchester man is the founder of the world-famous "Mayo Clinic".

The Atom was first split in Manchester. Ernest Rutherford moved to England from New Zealand after taking the position of Chair of Physics at Manchester University. In 1917, he disintegrated the nuclei of nitrogen atoms by firing particles from a radioactive source at them. This was the "splitting the atom" in a nuclear reaction between nitrogen and alpha particles, in which he also discovered (and named) the proton. It's also the world's first ever artificially-induced nuclear reaction, and it was a breakthrough that would eventually lead to nuclear power and the development of atomic bombs.

Industrial Revolution. Manchester is known as the Birthplace of the Industrial Revolution. Therefore, the worker bee is the symbol for Manchester because the bee represents industry. Manchester is technically a twin city, just like Minneapolis-St. Paul in Minnesota. Manchester's

twin is Salford, which is now part of Greater Manchester county. The bee first appeared on the Salford City Coat of Arms, and it was then adopted during the Industrial Revolution to symbolise the hard work ethic of Mancunians during the 19th century. This is because during that time, Manchester was literally a "hive" of activity as the world leader in mass production. You will see the "bee" symbol throughout Manchester, on potted plant pots, garbage bins, murals on walls, as badges on cars, and on the tile floors of the Town Hall.

Joseph Whitworth. He was an engineer who invented the standardization of all threads on nuts, bolts and screws. Prior to his universal standardisation, true mass production wasn't possible. This was because every manufacturer would use their own arbitrary thread sizes. Whitworth Hall and Whitworth Street in Manchester are both named after him. He was born in Stockport, Cheshire, which is part of the enormous county of Greater Manchester.

Karl Marx met Frederick Engels. Karl Marx and Frederick Engels would meet at the Red Dragon pub in Salford to discuss socialism and capitalism over drinks there.

Nigel Martin-Smith. After the success of New Kids on the Block of the United States, Nigel Martin-Smith formed the British boy band "Take That".

Bridgewater Canal. The Bridgewater Canal was the first true canal in England, and it connects together Runcorn, Manchester and Leigh to the North West England.

John Dalton. He was born in Cumberland but moved to Manchester, and he's the chemist who is best known for his Atomic Theory, and research in colour blindness. His table of atomic weights is a major precursor to all modern chemistry.

John Alcock and Arthur Brown. John Alcock was born in Manchester and Arthur Brown in Glasgow, Scotland. Brown's parents were American, and soon after he was born they moved to Manchester. In June of 1919 the Alcock and Brown became the first people to make a non-stop transatlantic flight.

Emmeline Pankhurst. She was born in Manchester and was the leader of the suffragette movement. She was instrumental in helping women win the right to vote. This changed the status of women all over the world.

L.S. Lowry. L.S. Lowry was a famous artist who lived in Rusholme, a suburb of Manchester. This was also where my husband Brian grew up. Lowry moved to Pendlebury in Greater Manchester with his parents at age 22, due to

financial difficulties. Brian has an L.S. Lowry picture in our living room, and it's fascinatingly beautiful. Strangely, the gentleman in the centre of the picture reminds him of his Father, so it's very special to us. Even the street that Lowry painted looks exactly like the one where his Father was born and grew up living on.

Alan Turing. Alan Turing in 1936 wrote the first published paper, "On Computable Numbers, with an

application to the Entschediungsproblem". This became the foundation for all Computer Science as we know it today. "Baby" was a nickname for the first Small-Scale Experimental Machine (SSEM) built in Manchester, and this machine was the basis from which all modern computers originate from. There is a replica of

PAINTING IS LOCATED IN THE GREAT NORTHERN BUILDING IN MANCHESTER, PHOTO BY HELEN WUORIO

"Baby" at the Museum of Science and Industry in Manchester. Alan Turing is also the person who broke the

55

Enigma code at Bletchley Park during World War II. Historians estimate that the amazing Manchester-man, Alan Turing, made a breakthrough discovery that shortened the war by as much as 4 years, and in doing so, saved the lives of as many as 21 million people!

Noel and Liam Gallagher. Noel and Liam were born in Manchester and were part of the famous British music group, Oasis. Noel and Liam went to the same High School my husband went to, which is Burnage Academy for Boys.

PAINTINGS LOCATED AT THE GREAT NORTHERN BUILDING, MANCHESTER, ENGLAND. PHOTO BY HELEN WUORIO

Benedict Cumberbatch. He of course is the actor that plays "Sherlock Holmes" and has been in many other films, most recently, "Dr Strange". Technically he is not from Manchester, but he did attend the University of Manchester.

Chapter 8: Christmas Crackers

In late November 2016 we arrived in Manchester, and instead of going to sleep after our transatlantic flight, we decided to stay up all day to try to get into the correct

sleeping schedule to help beat the jet lag. Since it was getting close to Christmas, we decided to visit the

BRIAN BEING CHEEKY AGAIN AT THE CHRISTMAS MARKETS

Manchester Christmas Markets in the city centre. I had never been to a British Christmas Market before, and it was absolutely stunning. The markets had taken over almost all the pedestrian streets in the city centre, and they were packed with beautifully themed small wooden chalet's. Each one also perfectly complimented the regular stores which were also preparing for Christmas around Albert Square and St. Anne's Square. There was mulled wine, roasting chestnuts, and you could feel the genuine holiday cheer everywhere throughout the city.

Once I'd experienced the Manchester Christmas Markets, I realized that the celebrations back in Minnesota don't even come close in comparison. In Minnesota, we used to have the Holidazzle Parade, and the Macy's 8th Floor Christmas Display, which were a wonderful tradition for my family, but sadly they don't do these anymore. The city of Minneapolis tried to reinvent a smaller-scale Christmas Holidazzle Market, and the previous year I had taken my husband to see it. He was less than impressed. I think he used words like "non-event" and "inept", and I can see why now. He was used to visiting the spectacular Christmas Market events in Manchester, and all he was faced in Loring Park Minneapolis was a small gathering of tents and less than imaginative supporting events.

I'm sure that many people can relate to suddenly receiving a barrage of text messages the moment you

 switch on your cell phone after a long flight. Landing in Manchester this Christmastime was no exception, and one message in particular caught my attention. It was from a friend in America who had asked me to get him some Christmas Crackers and post/mail them to him. Naturally, I thought to myself that while we're at the

Christmas Markets I'd almost certainly find Christmas Crackers for sale there, whatever they were. I had naturally assumed that they must be some sort of special tasty cracker that you can only get in Britain at Christmastime. I looked all over for them, and thoroughly checked each stall we visited. By the end of the afternoon I hadn't spotted a single Christmas Crackers. "Oh well…" I thought I would just have to keep looking for these elusive treats when we go to a shopping mall or department store.

VONNIE (SEATED) WITH GERRY AND ME PULLING MY FIRST CHRISTMAS CRACKER

A few nights later we decided to stop at our friends Vonnie and Gerry to visit with them. I just adore visiting with Vonnie and Gerry and hearing about all their stories from their acting days in major movies and stage shows. The number of A-list celebrities these guys used to work with, and are still friends with, never ceases to amaze me. Towards the end of the evening, Vonnie asked me if I would like a Christmas Cracker. Finally, I would get to try one of the infamous Christmas Crackers. When I said, "Sure, I'll try one.", she looked a little confused, and went into the other room. I was expecting her to come back with a tray of cheese and crackers, however, instead she comes out with a brightly decorated paper cylinder wrapped package. I naturally enquired what this was, when she asked me, "Haven't you ever pulled a Christmas Cracker before?"

I was the subject of some fun and teasing for a few minutes, but I didn't mind. I was just relieved to find out what these things really were. I'd never have even dreamed that they wouldn't be some sort of food, and that they'd be a fun type of party game. Two people hold opposing ends of a Christmas Cracker, and then pull it apart. As it's pulled it releases a small firecracker inside the paper cylinder, which makes a cracking, popping, and/or snapping sound. The person left holding the larger portion of the paper cylinder wins the prizes inside. These typically include a fun paper party hat/crown which you must wear, a toy or useful gadget, and an obligatory joke which you must then read aloud to your fellow party goers.

I was hooked, and naturally I had to include this curiously British tradition in this book. The Christmas Cracker tradition was started by a gentleman named Tom Smith from London. Sometime between 1845 to 1850 he had seen the French "bon bon" which was wrapped in a cylinder shape and thought that he would try selling sweets like that in England, but also include a riddle with it. Unfortunately, they didn't sell very well.

The legend is that while he was sitting in front of a log fire, he was mesmerized by the cracking noises made by the wood on the open fire. Apparently, it was because of this that he then came up with the idea that it would be fun if he could make his paper wrappers crack when they were opened by pulling them in half.

After Tom passed away, his three sons took over the cracker business, Tom, Walter and Henry. Walter is responsible for the idea of adding the paper hats into the crackers, and as well as traveling all over the world to come up with new ideas of things to put inside the crackers.

It's an English tradition to have a Christmas Cracker at each place setting for Christmas dinner, and to open them before eating so that you can wear the paper crown, and to cause everyone to roll their eyes when you tell the corny jokes during Christmas dinner.

Chapter 9: Brits and Hoarding

Even though we own several properties in England, the one we chose to live in so that we could renovate it, was one that he had bought for his parents as a gift in the mid 1980's. Sadly, his Father passed away after enjoying their new home for only a couple of years, and his Mother passed away 21 years later in 2011. Since Brian was busy travelling producing major TV documentaries during those years, he had only rarely visited the place, and if he did, then it was for no more than a couple of weeks each year. Therefore, I wasn't too surprised to find that he'd never really got around to sorting anything out.

The place we inherited was not untypical of one which an elderly lady would live in, and it was full of memories, magazines, books, fine china, and curiously, lots of empty Remy Martin brandy tins. This was all very charming and sweet, but it also made things a little cramped, so we began slowly sorting through things to make the place our own and easier to live in. When you walk into the place, it's really is like stepping straight back in time back to 1979. It has a speckled glass wall in the bedroom, and a brown bathroom suite. This might have been trendy back in 1979 when it was built, but, it's hideous as a bathroom colour choice in 2018.

We decided to be drastic about it and drew up plans to renovate it dramatically from bare shell walls inwards. Originally, we were going to make it ultra-modern, but after we had visits from several contractors to get cost estimates, we're not so sure now. Everyone who has inspected the place so far have all been very impressed by the genuine overall retro look and feel, which apparently it is all the rage now. Such is life...

As New Year's Eve of 2016 approached, I was starting to feel a little less than festive, thanks to a tummy ache. Since I wasn't sure how sick I'd become, and feeling less well by the moment, I went to lie down for a while, hoping that the feelings of nausea would go away.

My husband had the bright idea of giving me some Milk of Magnesia tablets to help settle my tummy. I didn't see where he got them, and at that point I didn't really care because my tummy was hurting so badly. I put the tablet in my mouth thinking that it would dissolve. I waited a few minutes, and nothing was dissolving. I thought maybe I need to bite down on it to help it dissolve, but no, nothing. in fact, I almost cracked a tooth when I bit down on it! After about ten minutes of trying to get the tablet to dissolve, I finally gave up, placed it on the night stand, and proceeded to be quite ill for the next 12 hours. By now it was obvious that I had caught some sort of stomach bug. That was definitely not the most romantic way to ring in the new year. My husband was his kind, attentive, and basically his loving self as he took great care of me.

Eventually, the nausea began to subside, and I was able to sleep for a few hours. When I woke up, I was beginning to feel a little more human again. It was then that I noticed a little brown medical-style of bottle on the kitchen work surface, and it appeared to be very old. I picked it up and read the label, which said, "Milk of Magnesia". I quickly turned the bottle around and read the expiration date, which was August 1994! Are you kidding me?!! If they expired in 1994, when were these things bought, probably sometime in the late 1980's! My husband had given me Milk of Magnesia tablets that had expired over 25 years ago, in fact tablets that were so old they had literally turned to stone!

The very next day we went through all the medicines in the home and discarded of anything and everything that was expired, and there were a lot. It seems that the Brits, well, one Brit in particular, really do save everything and can be hoarders! To this day, I do not let him live this little escapade down.

Chapter 10: Size and Stats Can Matter

So far, I've told you a little bit about me, my husband, and shared a few funny stories about starting our Anglo-American life together. However, I've not talked a lot about the many language differences, cultural differences, and other quirky facts, figures and comparisons, so I thought that it was about time that I began.

The first thing that I thought I'd set into perspective was size. Before any people reading this with naughty minds can think differently, I'm naturally talking about the comparison size differences between our two countries.

Very few people in Britain have any real clue about how vast the United States is until, they visit there and travel around. To put it simply, the United States is a vast country, and if you're a Brit visiting, or moving there, then be prepared for some very long road trips. Conversely, if you're an American coming to visit or live in Britain, then you'll find it a very tiny country by comparison. My husband likes to call Britain, "Compact and bijou", but to me that sounds more like a term which a realtor in America would use, or the equivalent in Britain would be an estate agent.

To put the size differentials in perspective, the United Kingdom is a very small country, and the United States is virtually half a continent! The United States is 3.80 million square miles, or 9.83 million km², whereas the United Kingdom is only 94,058 square miles, or 243,611 km². This is a huge differential, because you can fit the U.K. into the U.S.A. no less than 40 times!

Comparing size is an interesting thing, and for those of you who are still dragging your thoughts out of the gutter about where I was going with this section, I'm now going to compare various American States with the size of the United Kingdom. For example, the entire United Kingdom is only 57% the size of the State of California, and the Lone Star State of Texas is 3 times bigger than the U.K.!

When I found this out, I decided to take my research a step further. I then discovered that the American State that is closest in size to England alone, is Alabama. The total land area of England is 50,345 square miles, and the total land area of Alabama is 52,419 square miles, making the two quite similar. The land area of the entire U.K. is 94,058 square miles, and the land area of Oregon is 98,466 square miles. Therefore, Oregon is the closest State in America to the size of the entire United Kingdom!

Since I was now intrigued by comparison, here are all the States in America listed in size comparison with the United Kingdom. If you're American, you can then clearly see how your State compares in size to the U.K., and if you're a Brit travelling to the U.S. then you can see how big the States are that you intend to travel to. The figures listed are approximate comparisons that are either rounded up or rounded down.

State in America	Comparison Size to the U.K.
Alaska	7 Times Larger
Texas	3 Times Larger
California	1.7 Times Larger
Montana	1.5 Times Larger

New Mexico	1.3 Times Larger
Arizona	1.2 Times Larger
Nevada	1.2 Times Larger
Colorado	1.2 Times larger
Wyoming	1.035 Times Larger
Michigan	1.03 Times Larger
Oregon	1.02 Times larger
Minnesota	0.92% of the U.K.
Utah	0.90% of the U.K.
Idaho	0.89% of the U.K.
Kansas	0.88% of the U.K.
Nebraska	0.825% of the U.K.
South Dakota	0.82% of the U.K.
Washington	0.755% of the U.K.
North Dakota	0.75% of the U.K.
Oklahoma	0.74% of the U.K.
Missouri	0.737% of the U.K.
Florida	0.70% of the U.K.
Wisconsin	0.69% of the U.K.
Georgia	0.64% of the U.K.
Illinois	0.62% of the U.K.
Iowa	0.60% of the U.K.
New York	0.58% of the U.K.
North Carolina	0.57% of the U.K.
Arkansas	0.565% of the U.K.
Alabama	0.56% of the U.K.
Louisiana	0.55% of the U.K.
Mississippi	0.51% of the U.K.
Pennsylvania	0.49% of the U.K.
Ohio	0.47% of the U.K.
Virginia	0.459% of the U.K.
Tennessee	0.45% of the U.K.
Kentucky	0.439% of the U.K.
Indiana	0.40% of the U.K.
Maine	0.38% of the U.K.

South Carolina	0.34% of the U.K.
West Virginia	0.27% of the U.K.
Maryland	0.13% of the U.K.
Hawaii	0.12% of the U.K.
New Hampshire	0.10% of the U.K.
Vermont	0.09% of the U.K.
New Jersey	0.089% of the U.K.
Connecticut	0.06% of the U.K.
Delaware	0.035% of the U.K.
Rhode Island	0.02% of the U.K.

Apart from geographical size, there were several other statistical comparisons between the two countries that I found very interesting. For example, on average a person would make about 30% less money if they lived in Britain, however, if they moved to America they would spend about 59% more money on health care. Therefore, when you compare the two, you'd be far better off financially living in Britain instead of in America. Amazingly, if you live in Britain you have almost 74% less chance of being murdered, and you'll be almost 83% less likely to end up in jail.

In addition to avoiding being murdered or ending up in jail, living in Britain will add just short of one year onto your overall lifespan. You'll also have about 8% more free time on your hands, and you're currently 1.5 times less likely to be unemployed.

Unsurprisingly, the Brits consume much less energy than we Americans. If you live in Britain, then you'll consume approximately 68% less oil than you would do if you lived in America, and you'll use an average of about 58% less electricity in Britain too.

Electricity in Britain runs on 240 volts, and in Europe and most of the rest of the world on 220 volts. Since the United States and Canada run on 110 volts, DO NOT bring over hair dryers and curling irons to Britain and just plug them in, unless you want them to literally explode in your hands!

You'll either need to bring a weighty travel transformer, or simply buy these things in Britain. Conversely, if you're a Brit who take these items with you to the United States, then they won't blow up, and instead they'll be running on half power, and at half efficiency.

This means that in Britain you won't find electrical sockets/outlets in bathrooms. This is due to the higher risk of death by electrocution from the higher voltages and amps used in Britain. It's important to remember that t's not the number of volts that will kill you, it's the amount of current, or amps that will.

The United States still uses 110 volts because of the DC power systems created by Thomas Edison, and because he chose 110 volts to power his electric light bulb. Whereas the British system today is essentially what the amazing Nicola Tesla suggested. He recommended that 60 Hertz cycles per second was the best frequency for alternating current, AKA, A.C. power, combined with 240 volts.

Chapter 11: Chip or Crisp?

The term "chips" and "crisps" are two of the most commonly confused terms that any Anglo-American couple will encounter. I thought it wise to tackle the subject head-on, together with several other commonly confusing culinary terms.

Fish and Chips. To Americans, chips are known as French fries, and chips are potato chips, which the British will always call crisps. If you ask for chips in Britain, then you will get served French fries. If you really want French fries, be sure to ask for chips. My husband rightly pointed out that even in America, they will serve fish and chips, and when they're associated with that dish, then we Americans somehow miraculously automatically know that chips are chips/French fries, and not potato chips/crisps.

In Britain, fish and chips are usually served with lashings of salt and vinegar, with a side order of mushy peas. When bought from a takeaway, (In America we would call it a 'take out') they're wrapped in a greaseproof sheet or are on a tray, and then wrapped in paper. Somehow, the paper wrapping seals-in the moisture and heat, which makes the entire dish taste much better than any we've ever had when served in a restaurant.

Depending upon which part of Britain you're in, fish and chips may also be served with side orders of either sweet curry sauce or gravy. When I was first offered these as an option, I was highly dubious, and asked my husband to choose for me because I couldn't make up my mind. In reality, I didn't really fancy either option. However, when I tried the sweet curry sauce he had chosen for me, to my great surprise it complimented the fish and chips perfectly. It was an amazing combination, as was the gravy option my husband had chosen. So, if you haven't already tried either of these delicacies, then they should be placed high on your list of "must-do" things to experience when you arrive in Britain. For the best experience, I highly recommend that you get fish and chips from a good takeaway, because restaurant-served fish and chips never seem to compare.

Indian Cuisine. Speaking of curry sauce, I'm surprised at how popular Indian food is in Britain. In fact, it seems to have become a modern British staple. In Manchester we're blessed to have the world-famous "Curry Mile" as a place to enjoy real Indian and Asian cuisine.

The Curry Mile is in the Guinness Book of World Records as the largest collection of award-winning Indian

restaurants outside of India, and there are about a mile of them, when you add together all the restaurants from both sides of the road. The Curry Mile is now one of our favourite "go-to" places when we go out with friends locally, and especially when we have visitors from out of town and across the Atlantic.

I had first become acquainted with Indian food back in Minnesota, but once you've experienced the "real deal" from The Curry Mile, then nothing else really comes close. For a while, we were lucky in Minnesota when we had a beautiful Indian restaurant open in downtown Minneapolis called, OM. The food was excellent and could have easily been mistaken for a meal from The Curry Mile, thanks to the great chef Raghaven Iyer. Sadly, I don't think that Minneapolis was ready for genuine first class Indian cuisine, and unfortunately, my favourite contemporary Indian restaurant closed. The only consolation for me was that I could find Raghaven Iyer's cookbooks on Amazon. That is, if I was ever to suddenly become a big fan of cooking at home, which is highly unlikely because both my husband and I have no interest in it, and much prefer to go out to eat.

Our personal favourite restaurant on the Curry Mile is the Shere Khan. My husband Brian has been frequenting this place for years, and first met the owners, and management back in the late 90's when he worked for the BBC. At the time, the restaurant had won a BBC award for excellence. To this day, the owners and management always greet him with such a genuinely warm welcome every time we visit, and now they greet me the same way.

In our opinion, the Shere Khan restaurant has the very best food, and serving staff, on the entire Curry Mile, so if you ever get the opportunity to eat there, you must. We're both certain that you never be disappointed.

Pudding. Now this is a confusing one. In Britain, pudding is pretty much any type of sweet or dessert. It's not the traditional pudding we American's think of, such as

chocolate, vanilla or caramel. In Britain, this would be a custard. The subject of pudding quite naturally also raises the question of the pronunciation of the word, caramel. It wasn't until it was pointed out to me that I realised that we Americans butcher the word. This is probably because of our seeming inability to pronounce the letter "A" in the middle of the word. For some strange reason an American will say "Car-mel", when the word is actually spelt "Car-A-mel". I've no idea why this is, but if you're American, then I urge you to have some fun and try saying the word, "caramel", aloud while also pronouncing the letter "A" in the middle. I imagine that most people who have just tried this little experiment will also have completely failed to pronounce the letter "A" in the middle of the word.

Back to the subject of pudding. The Brits have something called a black pudding, which is not really a sweet dessert type of pudding at all. Instead, traditional

77

black pudding is made with oats, and either pork or beef, mixed with animal blood added to give it the black appearance. Neither Brian nor I have ever tried one of these because we don't eat meat, other than fish occasionally, so we can't tell you what it tastes like, or even recommend it to meat eaters. The closest thing we Americans would have to this dish would be called a blood pudding, but this would be dependent upon where you live in the country.

No talk of British pudding would be complete without including the world-famous Yorkshire Pudding. The first time I heard about Yorkshire Pudding was during my first Christmas in Manchester with our friend, Jane Hughes.

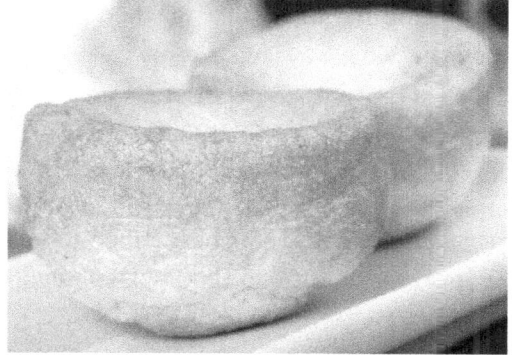

She was cooking a fabulous Christmas dinner for everyone, and when she said that she was also making Yorkshire Pudding, I naturally thought that she was making some sort of sweet dessert for afterwards. However, when she passed around a basket and asked if I wanted a Yorkshire Pudding, I was confused. It was then that I found out that a Yorkshire Pudding is what we Americans would call a "popover". A genuine Yorkshire Puddings is absolutely delicious, but it certainly wasn't what I was expecting at dinner that day.

Pies. Now that we have got the confusing subject of pudding cleared up, I'll confuse you even more with the subject of pies. A pie in England is traditionally not a sweet, or dessert, as we Americans would call it. Instead, a British pie can be filled with meat, potatoes, cheese, onions, and other veggies. A British pie is usually a savoury dish, and NOT a sweet. We Americans would perhaps call a British-style savoury pie a Shepherd's Pie, or a Cottage Pie, but that wouldn't really explain it. In addition, I didn't realize until I moved to Great Britain that a Cottage Pie is always made with beef, and Shepherd's Pie is quite naturally always made with lamb. This was one of my favourite things to eat that my mother made for me when I was growing up. However, we always mistakenly called the dish a Shepherd's Pie, because that was what our American recipe book had mistakenly called it. The Minnesotan version of that dish would perhaps be likened to Tator Tot Hotdish.

Now that I've just described the selection of savoury pies on offer in Britain, I'll now talk about the mince  pie. This isn't made with minced meat, instead, it's made with mincemeat, which isn't meat, or any other kind of animal product. Instead, it's made with chopped dried fruit, spirits, and spices, which when combined is called, mincemeat for mince pies.

Over the years, the mince pie has been known by several names, including, "Christmas pie", "mutton pie", and "shrid pie". Initially they used to contain meat, hence the name given to the filling that is still used today. However, the quantity of meat they contained declined over the years, until only the fruit and spices were left. Technically, some minced pies may still contain meat today if they have been made with beef suet. So, if you're vegetarian or vegan, then double check the ingredients of a pie before you eat it. Today, a British-style Mince Pie is typically a small individual sized pie, and not something that you would cut up and serve to multiple people, and they're traditionally served at and around Christmastime either as a snack or dessert.

Naturally, the Brits do also eat traditional apple pies, and other kinds of fruit pies, just as we Americans would. They also eat open topped pies with pasty crumbs, and these are called, "crumble", not a pie. They're traditionally served with custard, which is the hot, thick, liquid-type of sweet custard, and perhaps ice cream too.

Pasty. A Pasty is very similar to a pie, and it's made by placing an uncooked filling, typically of meat and/or vegetables, on one half of a flat shortcrust pastry circle, then folding the pastry circle in half to wrap the filling in a semicircle before crimping the curved edge to form a seal before baking. They are particularly associated with the county of, Cornwall, in South West England, and the Cornish copper and tin miners of the 18th, and 19th centuries.

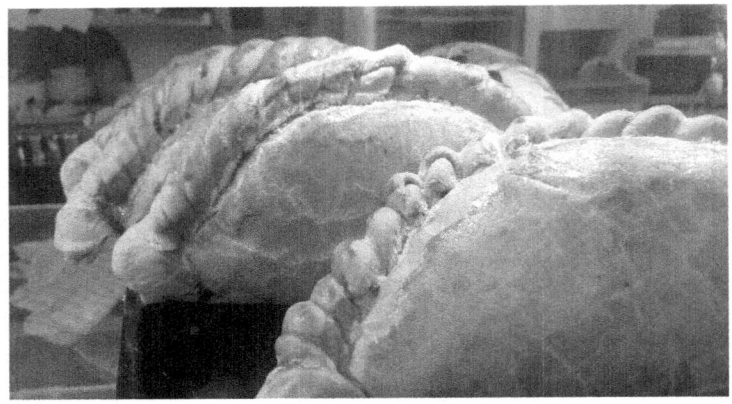

The side-crimping of traditional pasties suggested that the Cornish miner might have eaten the pasty by holding the thick, crimped edge of pastry, which was then later discarded to ensure that his dirty fingers, and possibly traces of arsenic form the mines, did not touch food or the miners mouth. However, during my research, many old photographs showed that pasties were also wrapped in bags made of paper or muslin and were eaten from end-to-end. According to the earliest Cornish cook book published in 1929, this is the true Cornish way to eat a pasty. Another theory suggests that pasties were marked at one end with an initial, and then eaten from the other end so that if the pasty wasn't finished at one mealtime, they could easily be identified later by their rightful owners.

The Cornish pasty is definitely one of our favourite foods when we're on holiday in our beloved Cornwall. We were also lucky to find a Cornish pasty shop in the fishing village of Whitby, in North Yorkshire, which is about 300 miles North and East of Cornwall. As well as serving traditionally savoury pasties, they also served a fabulous selection of sweet and fruit-filled versions. This was a gorgeous treat. FYI, "gorgeous", is another term British people use to describe delicious food, and I love to use this term now whenever I can, so of course I quickly and easily added it into my new, British-style daily vernacular.

English Breakfast. A traditional English Breakfast consists of 2 fried eggs, rashers of bacon, a sausage or two, half a tomato, mushrooms, baked beans and toast. This is a dish which is very common around Britain, and lots of hotels and guest houses proudly advertise serving a "Full English Breakfast" as part of their selling points.

Since my husband and I don't eat meat of course we opt for a vegan/vegetarian version of the same thing. Fortunately, Britain has a much better selection of

vegetarian and vegan options than are currently available back in the United States. At first, I thought it was a little odd to have baked beans with breakfast, but after living in Britain for only a short time, it doesn't seem right to not have them now. One of the best places to get a great Full English Breakfast in both vegetarian and meat-lover varieties, is at a Sainsbury's supermarket café. They serve one of the best breakfasts we've found so far, its inexpensive, and there are Sainsbury's supermarkets complete with cafés all over the country, so we highly recommend them.

Biscuits. What we call a biscuit in America is not the same as in Britain. As an American, I typically think of a biscuit as being a warm flaky type of bun that you have with dinner. Instead, a biscuit in Britain is what I would call a cookie back in America.

In Britain, it's very common to see biscuits dunked into cups of hot tea before being eaten. I had no idea that there were so many varieties of biscuits to choose from in Britain. There are McVities Digestives, Rich Tea, Hob Nobs, shortbread, Chocolate Bourbon, wafers, Garibaldi's, Jammie Dodger's, and the list goes on and on.

The selection was a bit overwhelming for me at first, and I genuinely wondered where I should start my exploration of these biscuit delights. Luckily my wonderful British husband has great friends, and the Hurst family comprising of Sharon, Stuart, Sophie and Oliver were only too willing to teach me the difference between biscuits.

Stuart Hurst is one of my husband's closest friends, and they are both martial arts experts. Since Stuart is a veteran two-time world Champion Thai Boxer, so the types and classification of biscuits he used were described to me in easy to understand martial arts terms.

Stuart then taught me the "martial art" of biscuit dunking, with everyone else laughing away while he did so. Apparently, mastery of the "martial art" of dunking a b scuit is clearly demonstrated when you're able to dunk a biscuit half way into a cup of hot tea, so that it becomes saturated to the point of falling apart. However, it's important not to let the biscuit actually fall apart, and instead, just before it does so, you must causally be able to lift it from the tea-dunked position and eat it normally. That sounded easy enough to me, but how mistaken I was.

The biscuits called Hob Nobs are technically the white belt of the dunking biscuit world. This is because they are a biscuit that a complete beginner can easily dunk, and they never fall apart no matter what you do to them. You can dunk one for quite a while and then take a bite, only to find that it's still crispy, so you dunk it again, and it's still crispy. You can dunk a Hob Nob long and hard you will almost never lose a single piece of it in your tea. They are the real tough guys of the biscuit world, and we even have coasters at home which we bought from The Royal Marines Shop Charity at the HQ in Plymouth which say, "Hob Nobs, The Royal Marines of the biscuit world!"

When learning the "martial art" of biscuit dunking, one must gradually work up to dunking a Rich Tea biscuit. This is because they are at the opposing end of the biscuit-dunking spectrum, and they fall apart almost immediately when dunked. Therefore, if you can master the art of dunking and successfully eating an unbroken Rich Tea biscuit, then you have earned your biscuit dunking "black belt". All other biscuits along the way are represented in martial arts-style colour grades of difficulty according to how challenging they are to dunk, and Stuart even devised a list for me to practice on at home. Homework never tasted so good before.

It was hilarious when we got together with the Hurst family for my "black belt" biscuit dunking test, because they had bought a complete spectrum of biscuit dunking challenges for me to try. I was feeling ready to be tested, because even if I failed, I still got to eat the biscuit and drink the biscuit flavoured tea.

Naturally, they started me with the Hob Nobs, and I passed that test with flying colours. Then we moved on to the McVities Digestives. You can dunk that biscuit for a reasonable amount of time and you usually won't lose a piece. However, you can sense the texture of the biscuit changing as you hold it, and when you place it in your mouth it is noticeably softer after only a single dunking. You would probably not want to double-dunk a digestive biscuit because you may lose a large piece in your tea cup.

I then rashly decided to bypass on the remaining test selection, and to just go for it, straight to the Rich Tea biscuit black belt level test. Our friends gasped jokingly, "Do you really want to go right for it?" I replied, "Yes! I can handle it!" There I go with the Rich Tea biscuit, I dunk it, then count 1 – 2 – 3, I then proceed to lift it to my mouth, and waiver for a second. Was the biscuit going to break? Would I get my biscuit-dunking black belt at my first attempt? Sadly, not. I'd waivered too long and had given the biscuit a little too much dunking time, so splosh! Half of the Rich Tea biscuit fell right back into my cuppa tea.

Darn it, I'd totally failed, and was then directly right back to the starting point, the white belt of the biscuit world, the delicious Hob Nobs. What a hardship... or not. Either way it was a delicious result, and one of those evenings spent with good friends when your sides hurt because you've been laughing so long and hard. I'm currently still only a biscuit-dunking white belt, but practice makes perfect I suppose.

Peckish. This is another British word I found funny. The first time I heard Brian say, "I'm a bit peckish", I had to laugh aloud. I was able to guess what he meant at the time, but the first thing that came to my mind was a chicken pecking for food. I assumed that he meant he was hungry, and the phrase was apt. I'd never heard that one before, and for some reason I still find it hysterical when I hear it. I almost had to bite my lip to prevent me laughing aloud at the wrong moments.

Courgette. I had seen this word on menus at several restaurants. Even though the dishes I saw which  contained them looked familiar, I was just too embarrassed to even ask what it was. I had never heard of that type of food before. The good news came just recently that I wasn't completely crazy, because a courgette is what we Americans would call a zucchini. Maybe I didn't recognise them when I first saw them because I really don't cook at home very much, and I hardly ever watch cookery shows on TV, but at least the mystery of the courgette was solved.

Toad in the Hole. This is a traditional English dish that consists of sausage and Yorkshire Pudding. I've never  tried the meat-lovers version, but if it's only half as delicious as the vegan version, then you won't be disappointed. Where I grew up in the Midwestern United States, a Toad in the Hole was a fried egg cooked in the middle

British Toad in the Hole
Photograph taken by Robert Gibert

87

of a piece of bread. This is quite different to the British version, but the principle is still the same and it's equally yummy. The origin of the name "Toad in the Hole" is a little hazy. However, written records of it go back to as far as 1762, and the name probably originated due to the sausages poking through the gaps in the batter.

Marmite. The manufacturers openly admit in their commercial advertising that "You either love it or hate it.", and that's about right. I haven't been able to bring myself to even try it yet, because just the thought of it alone is daunting enough. It's some type of dark brown paste-like spread made from yeast extract that tastes very salty. It's basically a by-product of brewing beer, and similar products on sale globally include the Australian Vegemite version.

Marmite
Photo by Malcolm Farmer, 28 June 2003

The yeast extract paste was first invented in the late 19th century, when German scientist called Justus von Liebig discovered that edible brewer's yeast could be concentrated and bottled. This discovery inspired people in Britain who loved it, and in 1902 they formed the Marmite Food Extract Company in Burton upon Trent, Staffordshire, which is about 75 miles South East of Manchester. Despite its continuing popularity here in Britain, I think I'll continue to pass on this one for now.

Spotted Dick. You can imagine the look of horror on my face when I first "spotted" this on the menu – sorry for the pun, but I couldn't resist! I thought to myself, "What in the world is that? Why would anyone want to eat something by the name of Spotted Dick?" I had to research this one, and

British Spotted Dick
By Tracy - Flickr: Contents of what was in the can, CC

unfortunately, I didn't find too many answers as to how it came by the name, and why it stuck.

Spotted Dick is a dessert pudding that is almost like an angel food cake made with suet and sprinkled with raisins and/or currents. It's then typically served with British-style hot liquid custard, which is yummy.

To make it, you'd take a flat sheet of suet pastry which is sprinkled with the dried fruit, and then rolled up into a circular pudding shape and cooked. I suppose that the dried fruit punctuating the dough is why it's called "spotted", and I can only imagine that the rolled-up pudding shape suggesting the rest of the name... I was being facetious there, because there seems to be a logical answer as to why it is called "Dick".

I discovered that in 19th century Britain the word "Dick" was a widely used slang term for pudding. This is very possibly a corruption of the Dutch word for dough, which is "deeg". A glossary of local terms used in and around the Yorkshire town of Huddersfield described "Dick" as plain pudding, and if it was served with treacle, then it would be called "Treacle Dick".

The first recorded use of the name was in The Pall Mall Gazette in 1892 which reported on a news story that "The Kilburn Sisters ... daily satisfied hundreds of dockers with soup and Spotted Dick." I shudder to think anything more about that article, and what the Kilburn sisters were serving. It shouldn't be at all that surprising that in Britain, the name "Spotted Dick" seems to have become thoroughly woven into the double entendre style vernacular the Brits seem to love so much.

Aubergine. Once again, just like with a courgette, when confronted with the word "Aubergine", I had a completely blank expression on my face. Just like before, I had absolutely no idea what an  aubergine was until recently when I discovered that it was what we Americans call an eggplant.

Jacket Potato. A jacket potato is the same as what we Americans call a baked potato. These are immensely popular in Britain, and they love to dress them up with all kinds of delicious toppings such as tuna and mayo, sweetcorn, baked beans, chilli, cheese and onion, or whatever else you can think of. It's quite an imaginative selection when compared to being back in Minnesota, where we would typically just put butter and sour cream on a baked potato. The first time I heard the term "jacket

potato" I pictured a potato walking around in a jacket, but that's just my silly sense of humour and over-active imagination working overtime.

My absolute favourite place to get a jacket potato, and you may laugh here, but it's at Costco wholesale in Manchester, near The Trafford Centre shopping mall. They serve the best tuna and mayo jacket potato at the café for only £1.50! Seriously, these are the best jacket potatoes, and the best value, you'll find anywhere. Apparently, I have the inability to say "tuna" properly. It always comes out as "toona" and I ALWAYS get a look of utter confusion from the lady behind the counter.

Treacle. Treacle is what we Americans would call Molasses. A sticky dark syrup made from refined sugar.

Candy Floss. Candy floss is what we America would call cotton candy. It's made in the same way, which is basically a form of spun sugar with some flavouring and food colouring. In Australia it's called Fairy Floss.

Sweets. Sweets in Britain are basically any type of candy. In recent years, especially in small rural and seaside villages, you'll find cute little sweet shops where sweets are served directly from large jars and then weighed to order, just like in the old days. I even remember these types of shops in the 70's in Duluth, Minnesota as the "penny candy store".

Ice Lolly. An Ice Lolly is either an ice sorbet, or flavoured ice cream on a stick. In the United States we would call it a popsicle. Variations on the theme include chocolate-coating the ice cream or making it all dairy-free.

Butty and Sandwich. A "butty" is a British slang term for either a filled, or less typically, an open face sandwich. Often in Britain, they even fill them with chips, AKA French fries, to create the famous "chip butty". A slang term for a particularly large butty, or sandwich, would be a "dockers wedge", probably because of the particularly thick wooden wedges used on the docks to stabilize goods in transit by sea.

92

Before being known as sandwiches, this combination of bread and food was simply known as "bread and meat", or "bread and cheese" if cheese was the filling. The word "sandwich" comes from John Montagu, 4th Earl of Sandwich (1770 to 1771) who was an eighteenth-century

English aristocrat. Lord Sandwich was particularly fond of playing cards, and especially cribbage. He loved this form of food because it allowed him to continue to play cards while eating without needing a knife and fork, and without getting his cards greasy from eating meat with his bare hands. It is rumoured that when the Earl Montagu ordered his valet to bring him meat tucked between two pieces of bread, and others who were with him at the card table began to order, "The same as Sandwich!", and this ancient form of food was at last christened with a name.

Apricot. One day, I had asked my husband, Brian, if we could get some apricots, pronouncing it "a-prə-ˌkät" of course. He just stood there and looked at me with an expression of utter confusion on his face. Initially, he couldn't for the life of him understand what I was saying until he finally realized I was saying apricot. The way Brits pronounce the word which would be "AY" + "pruh" + "kot" or variations on the same. It's almost like I learn something new about our commonalities and differences every day.

Potluck. I soon discovered that this is not a British thing, it's almost exclusively American. I was chatting with my British friend Sharon one day, and we got to talking about Super Bowl parties and how we always have a "Potluck" to accompany them. She had absolutely no dea what I was talking about. Even though she had visitec us in the United States on many occasions, the term "potluck" must have escaped her, because she had never heard of it before. A "potluck" is when all your guests bring a dish of their choice to share, and which is entirely at random. In England they might at best say, "Please bring a dish to share", because they do not have a specific word for it

Jelly. In Britain, "jelly" is a gelatine-based dessert which we Americans would call, Jell-O. Jell-O is a trademarked brand which has become synonymous with the product and is a proprietary eponym, in the same way that a Kleenex is now often used to describe many types of facial tissue.

Bubble and Squeak. They really have some of the oddest names for food here in Britain. Bubble and squeak is made from the leftover vegetables, mostly potatoes, cabbage, and pretty much anything else that is leftover, usually from a Sunday Roast. The vegetables are then fried together in a pan, and the name comes from the sound of the cabbage which bubbles and makes a squeaking noise when being cooked.

Chapter 12: Heartbeat TV Show

One day while we were trawling through some of Brian's collection of old movies and TV shows, I found something that caught my eye. It was a complete set of the

classic British TV show called "Heartbeat" which was fimed between 1992 and 2009 for 18 seasons. It's set in the 1960's, and it's about a police officer from London who moves with his wife, who is a medical doctor, to a small country village in North Yorkshire, which is the area where his wife was born.

I thought that we'd give it a try one evening, and even though I initially found some of the accents a litt e hard to follow, after the first few episodes I was hooked. I completely fell in love with several of the characters including, "Greengrass", played by actor Bill Maynard, and his dog Alfred, "Sergeant Blaketon", played by actor Derek Fowlds, "Nick Rowan", played by actor Nick Berry, anc "Gina Ward", played by actor Tricia Penrose.

The show is set in the fictional village of "Aidensfield", which is really the village of Goathland, set deep in the North Yorkshire moors. It's a beautiful little village, and a perfect place to visit for a day out. The locals must have grown to love and embrace the TV show because they have even preserved the classic 60's police car used in the show, which is now situated outside the local village shops. When we first visited there, the village was exactly like stepping back in time, into the film set for the TV show. Occasionally while daydreaming, I even half expected to see some of the characters from the show walking down the street, or calling into the local pub.

It is because of this show that I first learned that British Police Officers are sometimes referred to as "Bobbies". After a little research, I discovered that the term "Bobbies" is occasionally used about the police because of the contracted first name of the man who organized the World's first police force in London in 1829. His name was Sir Robert Peel, AKA "Bobby". The organization turned out to be a success, and from then on, Police Officers were then often referred to as either "Peelers", or as most people know them today, "Bobbies".

I was surprised at just how warm and friendly the

 "Bobbies" are in Manchester, and that they were even genuinely happy to stop and let me pose for a photo with them by a patrol car one day while we were in town.

One evening we had spotted some very suspicious looking teenagers lurking around some private grounds near to where we live. Brian called the police to alert them. In Britain, if you need to call either the Police, Fire Department, or Ambulance Service, then you dial 999, and not 911 like you would back in the United States. When they arrived, I was taken aback at just how warm, friendly and polite the police officers were.

They looked around, but found nothing, and said they'd alert the local patrols in case they spotted anything suspicious. While they were taking details, Brian invited them inside our home, which once again surprised me because this is something that I'd never have done back in the United States.

While they were taking notes, Brian even offered them a "cuppa tea" which was gratefully accepted, so they sat down on the sofa and wrote notes while they all drank tea. I couldn't help thinking to myself, "How very Brit sh all of this is, it's just like I imagined it to be."

This whole scenario was entirely different to anything I'd experienced previously. In the United States, if an officer visited your home because of a similar incident, they would never accept an invitation to come into your home, sit down to make notes over a "cuppa tea", coffee, or anything else for that matter.

On the rare occasions I've needed to call the Police back in the United States, or have witnessed them helping someone else, officers there are usually much less friendly and community-spirit oriented. The British police get my vote now, thanks to their warm and friendly professionalism, and for their community spirit.

In the "Heartbeat" TV show, the two main characters, "Nick" and his wife "Dr Kate Rowan", move to the fictional village of "Aidensfield". "Dr Rowan" then made enquiries about working at the local surgery. This confused me. When I heard that, I just thought to myself that she must be a surgeon. I found

this a little odd, because in the United States you'd never find a surgeon and an operating theatre in a tiny village. However, after watching a few more episodes of the show, it finally dawned on me that in Britain the word "Surgery" is the common word for the doctor's office, or clinic. Now it all made sense. In America, we only use the word "surgery" when someone is going in to have a surgical procedure performed.

In addition, the Brits have a very different way of talking about people who are in the hospital. In America we would say that "Our friend is in the hospital.", whereas in Britain, they would say that "Our friend is in hospital." You would drop the word "the" entirely.

Luckily for me I'd already watched several episodes of the Heartbeat TV show before my first trip to England. Therefore, I'd already become accustomed to many of the terms used in the show which are still in common use in Britain today.

Another medical-related term which might cause some confusion is what the British people call a pharmacy. I remember the first time that we drove by our local pharmacy, and even though we passed this place regularly, for quite a while I didn't even realise that it was a pharmacy. This is because the sign outside merely says "Chemist" and nothing else. When I see the word, "Chemist", then in my mind at least, the first thing I think about is the movie image of a mad scientist in the building, creating potions and concoctions... There again, maybe I've just watched too many movies.

It was while watching the "Heartbeat" TV show that I first heard the term, "Lollipop Man". At the time, this term made no sense to me whatsoever, so I didn't take much notice at first. My favourite Heartbeat character, "Claude Jeremiah Greengrass", played by actor Bill Maynard, is always trying to make a quick buck, and when you first start watching this show he annoys you. However, after only a few episodes he grows on you, and you soon learn to love him, and of course his beautiful dog "Alfred".

"Alfred" is a Bedlington-whippet, and now any time I see a dog like that I always stop to pet it, and hopefully cuddle up with it. Yes, I'm a real dog-lover. I digress, here from my main anecdote, and also fully realise that dogs have nothing to do with the "Lollipop Man" story, but they are so adorable, so I thought they are always worth a mention. I'm sure that you'll agree with me.

Anyway, back to the explanation of what a "Lollipop Man", woman, or person is. In the TV show, "Greengrass", became the local "Lollipop Man" in the episode, "Kids". I'd never heard that term before and thought that maybe it was just something funny the writers had written into the TV show. Nope, I was wrong, and "Lollipop Man" is a real term for a real job in Britain. In the United States we would call a person who did this same job, a "crossing guard". Whereas in Britain, they are affectionately called "Lollipop Person", because of the large traffic warning sign they carry that in many ways does look like a huge lollipop.

Chapter 13: Queue/Car Park/Petrol Station...

Queue. When it comes to standing in line as we do in America, nobody here in Britain would say that. They'd even think you to be a little strange, and perhaps give you a slightly suspicious look if you were to ask, "Is this the line?", when referencing where to stand and wait in turn. I once had a woman say to me, "Oh, you mean the queue? Yes, this is it." Initially, her response took me by complete surprise because

we would never say that in the United States, at least in the part of the country I'm from in the Northern Midwest.

The literal dictionary definition of the word, queue is, "A line or sequence of people or vehicles awaiting their turn to be attended to or to proceed". So, the term is correct in respect of what it's used for, so it's curious why we Americans don't use it.

The word, queue, is borrowed straight from the French word queue, which itself comes from the Latin word cōda, which means "tail". Interestingly, in the mid-18th century a "queue" was a plaited-style of pony-tail worn by men, and they were even required dress-code for soldiers in the British army. Thankfully, this curious rule about plaited hair for soldiers only lasted about 100 years. Therefore, since the word, "queue", literally means, tail, it's almost always used when referring to a line of people waiting patiently in turn for something. In Britain, the term is also widely used in road signs, and if you ever visit the country and drive a car here, then you'll frequently see road signs saying things like, "Queueing likely" or "Queue Ahead".

Car Park. In Britain, you'll probably never see a sign saying, "parking lot", "parking spot", or "parking ramp", and instead you'll simply find signs for, "car park". Another term which might be used is, "garage", about the location being a public multiple parking garage. I'm not certain, but I believe that the term "parking ramp" might even be a Minnesota, or midwestern colloquialism.

Petrol. When you're in Britain, don't even think about asking for a gas station, because if you do, then you'll

just get a blank stare in return. In Britain, gasoline, AKA gas, is always called petrol, hence the common term here which is, petrol station. This is where you'll fill-up your car with fuel. In Britain, petrol, is a contraction of, petroleum spirit, or refined petroleum, which is what the product really is. Petroleum itself is simply the unrefined raw crude oil. In the United States we commonly use the term, gasoline, or gas for short, wh ch was first used in 1863, according to the Oxford English Dictionary, spelled "gasolene". The word "petrol" was first coined with the British around 1870.

If you visit Britain, and then ever decide to try out the Channel Tunnel to visit France, then it becomes even more confusing. This is because the French word, "gazole", which I admit sounds very much as though it should mean "gasoline", actually doesn't mean that at all. I've no doubt that many Americans have been caught out by this confusion when fuelling their hire car in France. In France, "gazole", refers only to diesel fuel, and not gasoline, so beware!

It's also important to note that back in America, the diesel pump almost always has a green hose and handle, however, in England, the green hose pump is for regular unleaded petrol, and not diesel. In Britain, the black hose and handle is always for diesel. Do not get the two mixed up, or you'll find yourself calling the car hire company (we would say 'rental car company') to arrange having your fuel tank drained. You'll also receive a very hefty bill.

In Britain, petrol is now sold by litres, and not by gallons. This is because of them still being part of the European Union, and this may change when Britain finally leaves. When you fill your car with fuel, you can estimate there to be about 4.5 litres to the gallon. Now, there's also the question of the size of a British Gallon, and an American Gallon, because the two aren't the same. A U.S. gallon is approximately 3.785 litres, while a UK's imperial gallon is approximately 4.546 litres. Many people get confused when comparing the fuel consumption figures of various vehicles on both sides of the pond. An American car, with figures quoted for the United States will be using the smaller gallon for the fuel consumption tests, therefore, it will always appear to be less fuel efficient than a British car. Both measurements might be called a gallon, however, they're very different in physical volume so you're not comparing like for like.

Road Surface. The road surface is the pavement on a road in the United States, and what we Americans occasionally call a road pavement. This is not the same thing as pavement in Britain, which is what we Americans would call the sidewalk. Also, it's good to remember that in Britain, and especially in Manchester, I've often found the pavements to be particularly uneven, and in need of repair. It's not a good idea for women to wear high heels while walking around British cities, and especially in Manchester. It's strange that I should have noticed this fact about the sidewalks, or rather the pavements in Manchester, because many years ago when Brian worked with BBC TV News, he and his friend Stuart Hurst produced a TV news report on how the pavements were badly in need of repair all around the city. It seems that nothing has changed since then.

Motorway. A Motorway in the United States is the equivalent of a "highway" or "freeway". However, in Britain, the traffic laws are much more stringent than those in most of the United States. For example, you can't use or even hold a cell phone if you're driving a vehicle, unless it's on a completely hands-free system. If you do, then you'll be stung with a huge fine of up to £1,000 or more! So, be warned.

In addition, don't even think about passing a vehicle using the inside lane, which is the side nearest to the pavement or curb. This is strictly forbidden in Britain for safety reasons, and if you decide to try it, then once again you'll be facing a big-money fine. Many lane-weaving American visitors have learned about this law the hard way.

Many motorways in Britain are now "smart" in that they are computer controlled to monitor traffic volume, speed, and flow. They will automatically alter the maximum speed you're allowed to travel based on these factors. Any alterations in speed will appear on a clearly illuminated sign on gantries over the motorway.

Visitors to Britain who drive on the motorway will also frequently notice chevrons painted on the road surface in each lane. These are evenly spaced apart and are a great help judging a correct safety distance between you and the vehicle in front of you. The golden rule is to always keep a two-chevron distance between you and the vehicle in front of you. Once again, driving nose-to-tail isn't tolerated in Britain in the same way that it's typically overlooked in the United States.

Almost all British motorways have speed control cameras at critical points, so if you pass one while exceeding the speed limit, you, and/or your car hire company will receive a speeding ticket and it will be deducted from the credit card you used to hire your car with. More often, you'll find what are called "average speed cameras" which are used on most motorways and other busy roads in Britain. These are clever devices that measure your average speed between cameras, and if you reach the next camera too soon, it means that you must have been speeding, so you'll be ticketed and fined. With these devices, it's possible to receive a complete driving ban in a single journey if you repeatedly break the law!

In general, across Britain, all roads are heavily monitored by cameras that can read your car license plate, or registration number as the Brits call it, and this means that the national computer system can recognise which cars are being driven, and who owns them. The system also knows which cars have been taxed, and are insured, so that they're legally allowed on the road.

All police cars in Britain are equipped with this system too, which means that drivers here aren't pulled over by police to perform an identity check as often as we are in the United States, because they already know if the car has been reported stolen, who you are if you're driving it, or who you should be.

Driver's License. In Britain, this is called a "driving license", which are slightly different in their use and format, but are basically the same thing.

If you're driving a vehicle in Britain you're required to have your driving license, insurance certificate, and M.O.T. certificate with you. An M.O.T. is annual test your vehicle must pass to check its road worthiness and exhaust emissions etc. This is a required test for all vehicles over 3 years of age, because it helps to ensure that all vehicles used on the road meet the current road safety standards.

The British driving license isn't used as a form of I.D. as the American licenses are, so you will always need to carry your passport with you when you travel by air within Britain. Interestingly, unlike in the United States, British people and visitors aren't required by law to always carry a form of I.D. with them when simply walking, shopping, or out socialising. This is something that took a while in getting used to when I first visited Britain, and then eventually moved here. You'll almost never hear the British police ask anyone to "Show me some I.D.", because it's just not the way things work here.

Flyover. A Flyover in Britain is what we Americans would call an overpass.

Diversion. A diversion in Britain is what we'd call a detour. I have noticed that when there is a diversion in the United Kingdom, they don't leave you guessing, because they give you plenty of signs to re-route you.

This is very different to most of the United States. Brian and I once decided to take a road trip from Minneapolis to Duluth in Minnesota. Not too long into the trip we suddenly found the entire freeway closed in the middle of the day, so we had to follow the detour, AKA diversion. The problem was that once we'd followed the initial diversion signs from the freeway, they had no further signs to tell you where to go to re-join the freeway ahead. It was incredible. We, and the other drivers following us, were all left entirely to our own devices, and maps, if you had any with you. Thank goodness for GPS. This method of diverting traffic and then leaving people guessing seems to happen a lot in the Twin Cities area of Minnesota. When one road is shut down, they will divert you to another road, but that road could easily be shut down as well, and/or there will be no other signs to follow. Brian often jokes that U.S. road diversion planners must expect drivers to "Use the Force" (as in the famous sci-fi movie) to help find the correct route.

Road Construction Sign. Another British road sign that may cause you to double-take at, is the road construction sign. I always think that it looks like a man struggling to open an umbrella. Whereas, it's supposed to look like it a man with a shovel who is shovelling dirt. Maybe it's  just me with an unusual sense of humour, but when you drive here, then you'll soon see for yourself.

Route. This one is the same for the U.K. and the for U.S., however, the difference is how we Americans say the word. We'd tend to think there are two ways of saying it, either, ROWT, or ROOT, depending upon when/how we use the word, such as in the title of the song, "Route 66".

In Britain, they will look at you as though you're crazy if you say "ROWT" instead of, route. Brian has often

pointed out to me that you wouldn't say that you're performing a workout "ROWTINE" because it would be silly. Then, why do we say "ROWT" since there isn't the letter "W" in the word? It makes sense when Brian explains it, and I am

genuinely not sure why we Americans get so confused with this one.

Windscreen. Windscreen is what we call a Windshield on a vehicle, so, there's not much difference there then.

Indicator. The indicator on a car is what we would call the blinker. I'm almost certain that we call it by that

name because it describes the action of what it does when you activate the indicator lever on the side of the car steering wheel.

Tyre. A tyre is of course a ring-shaped component surrounding the rim of a vehicle's wheel to transfer a vehicle's load and drive, from and through the axle to the ground. In doing so, it provides the traction needed to move the vehicle. In Britain they call it a "tyre" and in the United States we would call it a "tire". In Britain, you would only spell it, "tire", if you were referring to feeling tired or sleepy, which makes perfect sense now that I think about it.

The only possible reason I can think of as to why we Americans might spell it that way, as if we were tired, might be a throw-back to the old days of wooden wagon wheels. In those days, when a traditional spoked wooden wheel was built, it would be fitted with a metal band around the entire outer edge. The wheelwright would first heat the metal so that when it was fitted around the wheel it would shrink as it cools to make a tight fit. The action of shrinking could be said to "tie" the wheel components together, making it the "tie-er" which might have been the origin of why we Americans spell the word the way we do now. Admittedly, this explanation is a long-shot which is almost certainly apocryphal, but it's the best that I can come up with.

Charabanc AKA Sharra-bang. This is a common term in Britain, and technically, this means a horse-drawn carriage with wooden seats that would transport multiple people. It was especially popular in the early 20th century to transport people to the country or the seaside for a works official outing or holiday. The word

111

is still used today in some parts of Britain, but now it would be referring to a coach, or bus traveling to a holiday destination, or for a chartered private excursion.

Caravan. In Britain, the word, "caravan", can mean a group of people traveling together, however, this isn't so common these days. It can also refer to a covered horse-drawn wagon which would be called a Gypsy caravan.

Today, a "caravan" refers to a vehicle equipped for living in. This is typically towed by a car as a trailer and is used for holidays. From the information I've gathered, caravans aren't especially popular with the majority of drivers on the narrow British roads because they almost always cause huge tail-backs.

Other forms of caravan in Britain would be a mobile home, a camper van, a caravanette, of the classic Volkswagen-style dormobile which was especially popular in the 60's and 70's.

Caravan Park. In the United States we would call this an RV Park, or a place to park Recreational Vehicles. In Britain, a caravan park is typically a field where cars towing caravans can park, usually close to a scenic location, where people can take short breaks or holidays. These places usually have facilities such as electrical power, running water, and sewage facilities provided for customers.

Manual Transmission. Most cars in Britain have manual gearboxes, although automatic has become more popular in recent years. I've no idea why manual gearboxes are so popular here, and even the people who use them regularly often seem to resemble someone stirring a bowl of porridge when they're changing gear. The Smaller engine cars in the U.K. are almost always manual transmission, except for the small electric cars. However, many of the larger luxury cars, and especially the Land Rover brand which we prefer, are now only produced with automatic transmission. I think this is a good idea, because as my husband points out, overall, automatic transmission is much more fuel efficient. This is because a human being will never always change gear at the perfect time according to acceleration, and revs. Many people also struggle with clutch control. However, a machine will always do these things perfectly, it will never get tired, and it will do everything at the optimum time. When taking an overview, the automatic transmission will always be more efficient.

Maybe he's right, or maybe he's wrong, or maybe the answer is somewhere in the middle ground, who knows. The important thing is that any Americans visiting Britain will not be allowed to drive a manual transmission car unless they are qualified and tested to do so according to their licence. If you're hiring (renting) a car during your stay in Britain, then be sure to clear up this important point ahead of time, either or you may find yourself either unable to drive, of without any valid insurance cover.

Trolley. A Trolley in America is something you would ride on, kind of like a train, or tram. The most

 famous of these would be the cable car trolleys in San Francisco. There, you can take the trolley through the streets and visit most of the main tourist attractions around the city. In Britain, a trolley is a shopping cart, or I guess any type of cart that you would push. I did see at Manchester Airport that what we Americans would call the luggage cart, were called trolleys.

I have to say, I did know this one before I even met my husband. This is because one of my closest friends I used to work with back in Eden Prairie, Minnesota was a lady named Sobia, and she was from Reading, England. Reading is a place not far West of London and pronounced "Red-ing". When Sobia and I became friends, we'd occasionally go shopping at lunchtime to either Target or Costco, and I always thought it was so funny when she would ask, "Do we need a trolley?" Therefore, I'd started using that term long before I'd even met my husband.

Jaywalking. In Britain you should expect to see jaywalking, because it isn't illegal here. This isn't quite as scary a prospect as it might first appear because the Brits are usually quite good at this, and they're sensible about when and how they cross in between traffic.

Dual Carriageway. The term "Dual Carriageway" would be the same as what we Americans would call a "Divided Highway" with a median. This would usually have two lanes, in both directions, with some sort of divider between the directions of traffic.

Lorry. Lorry/Lorrie or articulated truck is a Semi-trailer truck or "semi". I was very interested in this term because my dad was an Ice-Road Trucker, and I literally grew up around semi-trucks from being a small child.

More importantly, why in the world is it called a lorry? Even after performing some extensive research into this, it seems that nobody is absolutely certain.

The word could have come from the rail transport industry where the word "lorry" has been in use since 1938, and refers to either a goods wagon, or a large flat wagon. The word "lorry" was also used for a large horse-drawn wagon carrying goods.

Boot. The boot in the UK is what we would call the trunk of the car. In the UK when they had horse drawn coaches, the coachman would sit on a box carrying his boots. They always kept them with just in case of repairs, hence the term "boot" came into use.

Bonnet. The bonnet of a car is the metal hood of a car that you lift to get to the engine. This is not to be confused with a bonnet that you would wear on your head as my husband decided to wear to shock me during our visit to Walnut Grove in Minnesota, which was the home of Laura Ingalls Wilder who wrote the "Little House on the Prairie" books.

One theory about why the Brits call the hood of a car, a bonnet dates to the earliest cars that were produced. In those days the metal that was used to cover the engine was typically hinged and secured using a large leather belt or strap. These leather straps typically had large ornate buckles, and some believe that they resembled a decorative bow on a woman's hat or bonnet. This story is quite possibly apocryphal, but in the absence of any other plausible explanation, I'm sticking with it.

Pelican Crossing (Previously Pelicon). The Brits are famous for being animal lovers, but when I first heard the term "pelican crossing" it made no sense. To me, it sounded silly, and that it was a kind of crossing intended for the apparent abundance of walking pelicans they had in Britain! A little research revealed the real meaning of the term. A "pelican" crossing is an acronym for a light-controlled crossing for pedestrians to cross busy roads. This is how they came up with the acronym "Pelican" (Pelicon) - **PE**destrian **LI**ght **CON**trolled crossing, so it makes complete sense really.

ZEBRA Crossing. A Zebra crossing is also a pedestrian crossing but this one has the white stripes on the pavement so that it is like a Zebra. On a side note, if you are pronouncing Zebra as "Zee-Bra" this would be incorrect. The British say "Zeh-Bra". There are a few other words we pronounce differently but we will get to that later in the book.

Occasionally you'll also hear some people use the term "Belisha"' beacon or crossing. This is also a zebra crossing, but with the addition of an amber-coloured lamp in the shape of a globe on the top a tall black and white pole. It was named after Leslie Hore-Belisha, who was the Minister of Transport in 1934 when they added the amber beacons to pedestrian crossings.

Roundabouts. A roundabout in Britain are what we in America would call a "traffic circle". There aren't a great many in the United states yet, but the numbers are steadily growing. Since they're still new to many people in the United States you can clearly see how confused the average driver is with a roundabout if you're in the car behind.

These are one of the great transport-related ideas that Britain has exported to the United States in an attempt to reduce the gridlock and traffic chaos caused by America's excessive deployment of stop signs.

Stop Signs. in Britain, traffic won't always stop and wait at a stop sign, as it would in the United States. In Britain, if the road is obviously clear of traffic, then a vehicle will simply slow down while the driver looks each way, and then drive on. In America, at least in Minnesota I was taught that you must stop for 3 seconds at a stop sign before proceeding, even if there is absolutely no traffic around. If you don't fully stop, you'll receive a ticket if a cop sees you do that. You've been warned!

Traffic Lights. For some reason in America, we always seem to call these, stop lights. I think that this is terribly negative thinking because they're only a stop light for half of the time, whereas the other half of the time, they're a GO light.

In Britain, the sequence of traffic lights is slightly different to the United States. After you've waited at a red light, before it turns green, it will become both a red and amber light at the same time. At this point, you can't set off, you must always wait until there is no other light showing other than green.

Traffic feeder lanes. You won't see many traffic feeder lanes in larger British cities to help you make a right turn, which would be a left turn in the United States. Also, in America this would be a turn signal light, typically with an arrow pointing in the direction you would be turning.

Apparently, this is because many of the city councils are deliberately trying to congest the traffic to strengthen their argument about wanting to introduce congestion charging in certain parts of the cities at certain times. This is sad, because the strategy is so transparent, and they re creating much more air pollution in the process.

If you drive while you're in Britain and need to make a right turn where there's no feeder lane, then take a tip from the car in front of you and follow their lead. You'll probably only be able to legally get one, or perhaps two cars through at the most, on each traffic light change. Take care and keep your wits about you.

Turning on a Red Light. In Britain you cannot turn on left on a red light, like you can in the United States when you are turning right. If you do this while you're in the UK, then you'll almost certainly receive a costly ticket for your trouble.

According to my husband Brian, this is one of America's greatest transport-related ideas, and it should be exported to Britain, and everywhere else, just as in the same way that the roundabout is a great British idea that has now been exported to the United States.

Public Transport. People in Britain tend to use public transport far more than people in the United States.

In the United States, using public transport is often viewed as a class issue, and used by people that can't afford their own transport.

This is unless you're in a city such as San Francisco, where people of all classes will often ride the BART light rail, and the trolleys. Other than tiny pockets of public transport usage like that, it s really looked down on.

In Britain, it's refreshingly different in this respect. People of all socio-economic backgrounds will use public transport whenever it suits them, and without it being a class issue, and nobody would ever be looked down on for doing so. Public transport in Britain is a great equaliser, and you can have a homeless person hop onto a bus, usually for free, while at the same time busy professionals will be seated on the same vehicle as they move around the busy city centres. Busses in Britain, will almost always have comfortable seats, Wi-Fi, user friendly luggage places, and lots of space for baby buggies and wheelchair users too.

Trains are similarly equipped, and they're a far cry from those very basic versions of passenger trains we have in the United States. British trains are treated more like an airliner, with stewards, restaurant/buffet cars, roaming snack bars, friendly attendants and entertainment systems on board to help make the journey more fun. If you're going to be in one city for any length of time, and plan to use public transport, then it's a good idea to buy one of the saver tickets. They make travelling around a lot less expensive and eliminate the need to be sorting through coins in a currency that you have no clue about when you board a bus.

Commuters with longer distances to travel will be far more accepting of the various park and ride schemes most cities have. Commuters will simply travel so far by car, and then park in a large suburban car park before hopping onto the train, or light rail to complete their journey.

The greater use of public transport by all classes, has almost certainly been helped along by the size, or rather lack of size, of British roads and streets. As an American, when you first land in Britain this is one of the first things that you will notice. The roads are just tiny by comparison to those we have in the United States.

We Americans often forget why this is. We completely overlook the fact that British roads have typically grown organically from being nothing more than a dirt walking track several thousand years ago. Eventually, the walking track became a horse and wagon track between villages and settlements. These settlements might only have been 10, 20, or 30 miles apart, but they would have been a very long and dangerous journey back in those days.

When the Romans invaded Britain in 43AD, only 43 years after the birth of Christ, then the wagon tracks became arrow-straight Roman roads to enable chariots and armies to travel long distances at speed.

From these humble beginnings, the British road system began, and developed into what we have today. Now we have a mix of straight roads, crooked roads, tiny roads, and motorways, in fact, all kinds of roads. Most of these, especially those in the towns and cities aren't very wide. This is because the buildings had already been built hundreds of years ago, before they needed wider roads.

There are even many Roman roads which are still used today. They're now all tarmac covered high-tech highways, but they're still good. You can always tell a Roman road because it will be named "something" street, or way, such as Watling Street, or Fosse Way.

Pickup Trucks. The pickup truck which is so common in the United States is a real rarity in Britain. I'm not sure why the Brits aren't big fans of these, probably due to the size of the roads here. If you spot one on the road in Britain, then you can proudly award yourself 10 points

SUV. In Britain, they don't often use the term "SUV" and instead, tend to use "4-wheel drive", or a "4x4" if they have something like a Land Rover. You'll also see many more useful hatchback cars in Britain.

Motorway Services. In Britain there are motorway service stations at regular sensible distances apart, all along every motorway/freeway. In fact, you'd struggle to find a section of motorway/freeway where there isn't a fully equipped service station every 15 to 25 miles apart. This is good news for any of you who need to find frequent "relief" through using a loo/restroom.

In addition, the motorway services in Britain are excellent, and they're far better equipped than those you would typically find in the United States. In the British motorway services, you'll find high-end supermarkets like Marks and Spencer, together with a plethora of all the brand-leading food court shops and refreshment vendors.

Parking in a motorway services parking lot, AKA car park, is typically restricted to 2 hours. You can stay longer if you pay a small fee, or if you're staying in one of the motels which are also frequently combined into the services areas.

A warning about the price of fuel! For some crazy reason the cost of fuel for your vehicle at a motorway services will always be about 30% higher than elsewhere. Supermarkets, and especially Costco, offer the best deals of all for fuel. In the United States, the price differential isn't worth arguing about at the freeway gas stations.

I did hear a news report about why fuel is so expensive at the British motorway services, and the guy being interviewed was a transparent PR embarrassment. He was trying to convince the public that the prices are so high because of transportation of fuel by road. HELLO – your service station is situated on a motorway, and trucks carrying fuel must drive right past your services to get to places in cities and towns like a supermarket or Costco where it can be bought SO much cheaper.

Therefore, in respect of buying fuel for any vehicle you might hire in Britain, then plan accordingly so that you avoid filling up at rip-off motorway service gas/petrol stations at all costs.

Underground. When taking the subway in London you would call it the "underground", or more commonly by its nickname, the tube, whereas in New York, you would call the same thing, the subway.

The London Underground was the world's first underground railway, opening in 1863, with the original line

being now part of the Circle, Hammersmith & City and Metropolitan lines. The London Underground

HELEN, FIRST TIME USING THE LONDON UNDERGROUND

was also the first to operate underground electric trains in 1890.

Mind the Gap. When travelling by the underground you'll hear over the public-address system the world-famous phrase, "Mind the Gap", many times. This phrase has been used on the London Underground since 1969, and has now become a sort of tradition, or institution. You'll

clearly see the phrase on signs and placards all over the underground. If you really get into the swing of things, then you can even buy T-shirts and sweatshirts in souvenir shops with it proudly printed on them. On a slightly more serious note, having now ridden the London Underground several times, there can be some very awkward gaps between the trains and the platforms. Therefore, dare I say it? You bet I can! "Please make sure that you... Mind the Gap!"

Why do the British drive on the left side of the road/right side of the car? It may surprise you to learn that about 35% of the world drive this way. Mostly they are former British colonies, which makes sense since the British Empire was the biggest the world has ever known. However, many other countries do too, including Japan.

There are many good reasons why the British, and other countries do this. Typically, these countries were all once feudal, with mostly right-handed knights. Therefore, keeping on the right side made sense because it kept the sword arm free to either wield it, or show that it was free when you passed by a friend.

It's also much easier for a right-handed person to mount their horse from the left side, especially when wearing a sword which would be on the left-hand side of their body. Archaeologists have now discovered that even the Romans observed rules about keeping to the left while travelling, and Roman armies always marched on the left side. Pope Boniface VIII even went as far as putting this rule of the road into law in 1300 AD.

Fast-forward to the 16th century. This is the period when the number of horses needed to pull the ever-larger wagons grew in number. This meant that to keep the whip hand free, and to be able to control all the horses in the large teams, it made good sense to sit on the horse situated on rear left-hand side.

Since these large horse teams and wagons were well-suited to the expanse of the Americas, the technique emigrated to what would eventually become the United States. However, in Britain, there wasn't a big demand for the extra-large teams of horses, so the drivers there remained seated on the right-hand side of the wagon.

In the 1900's, London was suffering from massive horse-drawn traffic congestion. To help ease the confusion, a law was passed to make all traffic on London Bridge keep to the left-hand side. This became part of the 1835 British Highway Act, and it was then adopted throughout the British Empire which was at its zenith by this time.

So now you know why the British drive on the left side of the road, and the right-hand side of the car, and we Americans adopted the left-handed driving position. It's all because it made good sense at the time in history, and in the geographical places where these rules were adopted.

Chapter 14: Fancy Dress

Next, I'm going to talk about fashion, or rather, the common terms used in Britain vs. those in the United States. I had a few embarrassing moments during my transition to become half-American and half-British, especially when it came to clothing items and shoes. I'm sure there are many more differences which I've not encountered yet, and which you might find out for yourself, but the ones I've shared here will be a good place to start.

Fancy Dress. When we first arrived in Britain, unsurprisingly, I very soon became close friends with one of my husband's oldest and closest friend Jane Hughes. They have known each other for decades, and she's just an all-

around lovely lady. She's also an Anglo-American, who was born in Britain, but now lives half of the year in the United States, and the other half in her native Cheshire. This makes her a great go-to person for me now, especially when dealing with Anglo-American matters. One time, I was so excited to share with her that Brian was going to take me to London, so I could see Phantom of the

Opera which was playing at Her Majesty's Theatre on the world-famous Haymarket.

As you might imagine, I was very excited about this. I told her that I wanted to wear my brand-new fancy dress. Her response surprised me greatly, because instead of her being pleased about that, she had a look of sheer horror on her face. She then asked me, "Why, Why, Why, Why, on  earth would you want to wear fancy dress to see a show!?" (Imagine her saying this in a lovely British accent) Now, I was really confused.

I knew that London was one of the world's leading capital cities, and I naturally thought that many people would dress to impress when they went out to see a high-end show, at a high-end venue. Perhaps I was wrong... I then began thinking to myself that maybe people don't dress up for shows in London anymore, perhaps they're now a casual affair? I admit it, I was baffled.

Suddenly, Jane's Anglo-American head kicked-into gear, and then exclaimed, "Oh my gosh, you mean a fancy dress, and not that you're going in fancy dress?" It was suddenly clear that she had realised something that I didn't know anything about. It was the subtlety of wearing "a fancy dress" or "wearing fancy dress", because there's a distinct difference between the two.

Fancy dress in the United Kingdom means a "Costume", as in a Halloween costume when one might dress up as either Dracula, or Frankenstein. What I meant in saying "fancy dress" was simply a dress which is more fancy, elegant and special than what I'd normally wear every day. Perhaps an evening or cocktail dress. Once this minor, but very important point was cleared up, then we began chatting about the type of dress I had and laughed-off the misunderstanding. Jane was so relieved I was not thinking of wearing something like a Wonder Woman costume to go and see Phantom of the Opera at a famous London theatre.

This raises an important point to remember though. This is that when you're going to attend a special event in Britain, it's always a good idea to double check the dress code in advance. It's far better to suffer the temporary embarrassment of clarifying the point ahead of time, rather than finding out after the fact once you've arrived.

If you've ever watched the fabulous movie, "Bridget Jones's Diary" starring Renee Zellweger, and think back to the part when no one had told her that the fancy dress party had changed dress code. Well, if you don't clarify Anglo-American dress code matters ahead of time, it could easily be you who is dressed as the bunny, and not Bridget Jones!

Jumper. A jumper in the United States would be a sleeveless, collarless dress worn over a blouse. However, in

Britain a jumper is a pullover sweater. The word "jumper" comes from an obsolete term for a large, loose-fitting men's jacket called a jump. It seems that in Britain, the term just hung around even after the garment fell out of use.

Vest. A vest in the Britain is what we would call a Tank Top, or "wife-beater" in the United States. You can imagine the look on my British husband's face when I told him that we often call a vest a "wife-beater" in the United States. He did also ask me why the garment is called a tank top in America, because it has nothing whatsoever to do with a military vehicle.

Initially, I thought that the origin of the term "wife-beater" must have been a fairly recent one. Possibly because of the popular TV shows about crime which usually feature at least one article about domestic violence with the arrested perpetrator inevitably wearing a ribbed white blood-stained tank top.

A little research into the history of this term was a real eye-opener. Apparently, the term may be much older than our late 20th century and early 21st century junk TV and media. It seems that the term "wife beater" goes all the way back to the Middle Ages in Britain. In those days when a knight lost their armour during combat, they could often continue to fight-on while wearing only their under-vest. This undervest was made of chainmail, so it was well up to the task, and these knights were then referred to as a waif beater. With, "waif", referring to a lost individual or abandoned person.

Fast-forward to the 18th century, and we're st ll in Britain and Europe. By this time, people didn't wear armour, so the term "waif beater" no longer had any meaning. However, it seems that the term eventually changed to sound very much like "wife beater" and became linked to husbands who ill-treated their wives.

Fast-forward yet again to the mid-20th century United States, and in particular Detroit, Michigan. At this time, the local police arrested a man called James Hartford, Jr. for beating his wife to death, and the local news media aired the story for quite a considerable time. More importantly, they almost constantly aired a picture of Hartford when he was arrested, and lo and behold, he was wearing a nasty-looking stained tank top while they continuously referred to him as "the wife beater".

From that time onwards, all men that wore dirty tank-topped under garments were referred to as wearing "wife-beaters" and the term became embedded into history.

BTW. In Britain, the same sort of sleeveless button up vest that you wear with a three-piece suit is called a waistcoat, and not a vest.

Trainers. We would call "trainers", either tennis shoes or sneakers in the United States. "Trainers" comes from the fact that they are shoes which you would wear to exercise, or train in, which makes sense.

Braces. Braces in both America and Britain are something you wear on your teeth. An orthodontist would fit to straighten your teeth. Typically, you would wear braces for between 2-4 years depending upon how much correction you need.

However, in Britain, "braces" are also something to hold up men's trousers. They're worn over each shoulder and attach to the trousers by either a clip or buttons.

In America, braces are what we call suspenders. Whereas in Britain, suspenders are always an item of women's lingerie, the sexy little item you wear around your

waist under a skirt, with clips to hold up your stockings. This one minor difference in terminology could result in a hugely embarrassing situation arising. It could also spiral out of control to become a huge passion-killer, instead of an evening to remember!

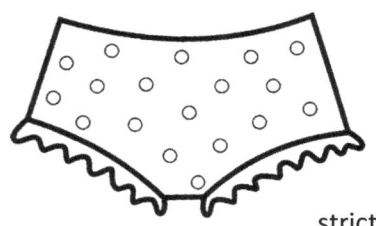 **Trousers & Pants.** You would never catch a Brit using the term "pants" instead of "trousers". In Britain, pants, or panties, are strictly women's underwear, or knickers. So, be extremely careful when going into a department store and asking for the pants section, they will direct you to the women's undergarments department.

Kecks. The word, "kecks" is a slang British plural noun for trousers. The word was derived from the archaic and now obsolete Northern English slang term, "kicks", which also meant trousers. "Trollies" and "strides" are two other British slang terms for trousers, and both are still used occasionally today. Whereas the slang term, "drawers", would mean the undergarments of either sexes, but more usually women's.

Bum Bag/Hip Bag. My husband and I always enjoy visiting renaissance festivals, and perhaps the best one of all is held for several months each year over summer in Shakopee, Minnesota.

Incidentally, in respect of the word "renaissance", an American would pronounce it, "REN-nay-sahnce", with the emphasis on the first three letters of the word. whereas, someone from Britain would say, "Re-NAY-Sahnce", with the emphasis on the second syllable. Back to the main anecdote after that short Anglo-American grammatical break.

We always dress the part when we attend a renaissance festival, so my husband usually brushes-off his kilt. It's a genuine heavy kilt, given to him by members of the Scots Guards regiment many years ago. I'd never known anyone to wear a kilt, but I  must say he looked very sexy to me. There's something very alluring about a confident man wearing a kilt... O.K., my daydream is over!

To his dismay, Brian discovered that he'd mistakenly left his sporran back in Britain, so he'd have to improvise if he was to be able to safely carry his wallet and cell phone with him. To him, the logical choice was to put a leather "fanny pack" on with the kilt instead. As he did so, I couldn't help myself and I laughed aloud as I said, "I haven't seen a fanny pack since the 80's!" Oh goodness, the look he gave me in response! He said, "You do know what the word 'fanny' means in Britain, right?" I looked at him completely confused, and replied, "Well, it means your rear-end, or butt, right?" He just shook his head in reply. Apparently, that is not what "fanny" means in Britain.

Brian exclaimed, "So, you're saying that I'm wearing a VAGINA Pack, right?!" In stark contrast to the meaning I had bestowed upon the word, to a Brit, "fanny" refers to the female genitals, and can therefore be considered highly offensive to many people in Britain. We both broke out into fits of  uncontrollable laughter about the mistaken terminology. It was then he explained to me that what he had decided to wear in the absence of his sporran, was what the Brits would call a "hip bag", or more commonly a "bum bag".

To make this crystal clear, in Britain, a bum, is a posterior, or rear end, and not a homeless person as we would think in the United States. In Britain, the commonly used word for a homeless person would be a "tramp".

Whilst on the subject of "bums", I thought that I may as well mention the word, arse. In Britain, this is a commonly used term for a rear end, bottom, or bum. If you're an American who is trying to say the word, "arse" as the Brits would do, then be sure to stress the letter R in the word, and not simply shorten it as we would normally to do to say, ass. If you did, then a Brit would immediacy tend to think of a 4-legged animal that goes "eee-aaw".

Swimming Costume. To me at least, the term, swimming costume, sounds like one is going to get dressed up in a fancy costume, such as a cartoon duck, or some other character. There again, I do have a vivid imagination.

I could also imagine that when we Americans say bathing suit, or swim suit, that some Brits are thinking to themselves, "Why would one go swimming wearing a 3-piece suit?"

A swimming costume is what you would wear to the beach to go swimming in. Unless of course you are in a Bikini Fitness Competition as I was, and then we'd call it a Competition Bikini Suit. Other than that, the terms for swimming costume, and bathing suit, are pretty much interchangeable on both sides of the pond.

This is me in my last competition, wearing a bikini, aka swimming costume, aka bathing suit.

Chapter 15: Anchors Aweigh!

Buoy. This is an interesting Anglo-American difference, and I'm certain that many people have encountered this on numerous occasions.

I was born and mostly raised in Minnesota, which is roughly in the central Mid-Western United States, and about as far from the ocean as you can get. However, Minnesota has a booming boating community thanks to the many lakes which are dotted all over the State. There are so many lakes in fact, that the nickname of the State proudly claims to be, "The Land of 10,000 Lakes". This is untrue, because the State has many more lakes than that. In fact, there are 11,842 lakes in Minnesota, and many smaller "almost-lakes" which are very large ponds, enormous in fact, but not quite large enough to be officially called a lake. These were the parting gifts of the enormous glaciers and ice sheets from the last great Ice Age, when massively thick sheets of ice covered a large part of what is now the United States.

Incidentally, I often laugh about Minnesota being "The Land of 10,000 Lakes" with my husband, because we often amuse ourselves by envisioning the person who had the job of officially counting them. More precisely, the various ways which last moment distractions might have occurred that may have caused them to lose count, so that they had to start the counting process all over again! These are just some of the silly games one plays to help stay alert when on the long road-trip drives across the vast States of America.

Naturally, with so many lakes, there will always be boats, and the people who love to mess about in them and have fun on the water. If you have boats, then as sure as night follows day, then you will also have buoys. This then begs the tedious question of how the word is, and more importantly, how it should be pronounced. Yet another Anglo-American conundrum.

Of course, the word, buoy, has the same meaning in both countries, which is a free-floating device in the water that can be anchored and used as a marker or anchor point. Thankfully, there's nothing different about that.

The big difference is in the pronunciation of the word. A typical American would pronounce it, "BOO-EEE",

whereas someone from Britain would say "BOI", or "BWY". Brian makes a good point here, he explains that you wouldn't ever say that something in the water such as a ship, or person swimming was "BOO-YINT" (Buoyant) because you would always say that they were, "BOI-YUNT", or "BWY-YUNT".

My husband Brian is a Master Scuba Diving Instructor (MSDT) with the PADI organisation, which is American-based. He points to their training videos which all clearly pronounce the word buoyancy one way, the way that they do in Britain. Yet, an American will immediately add letters to the word which aren't even in there when they try and pronounce the word for a single device called a buoy. Can anyone tell me where the letter "E" is in the word, buoyancy? It's simply not there, so I set about trying to research the origins of why we Americans add the letter when we say the word.

There wasn't much about this anywhere, which made it extremely frustrating. The only thread which made any sense, was that it's possible that in 1603 there was a mention in an old document that the word was sometimes spelled "bowie", which possibly indicates that this pronunciation existed in England at the time. If this is right, then it's also possible – *and this is where an already thin thread becomes even thinner* – that the way of pronouncing the word that way was brought over to the original British Colonies in North America with the Mayflower.

This is supported by my other research into the official origins of the word, which indicated the pronunciation might be from the Middle English words, "buoy", or "boye", meaning "a float". This could share roots from the Middle Dutch word, "boeye", which also means "a float, or signal", and the Middle French word, "bouee", or "boue", again meaning "a float, or marker, buoy". When one weighs these factors into the equation, it seems to me that the American pronunciation, or mispronunciation of the word, depending upon which way you look at it, could possibly go back to other European languages. Since the United States has always been a "melting pot" of the original British settlers into many other nations, and their languages, this all begins to make more sense.

When an American pronounces the word, "BOO-EEE", then for some reason they're almost certainly unconsciously feeling compelled to pronounce the word in some ancient British, Dutch or French style from the Middle Ages. Go figure that one...

This is a little like the way when Americans who are cooking and speak plain English when they're talking about ingredients. However, they suddenly convert to speaking French when they say the word, "herb", or "herbs" by dropping the letter "H" from the word completely. I'd never noticed this before until British friends who live part time in the United States pointed this out. Now I deliberately look out for it, and it's highly amusing to watch. It's almost like a scene from a comedy TV show where people don't even know that they suddenly start speaking a different language during a sketch.

Quay/Quayside. A quay is basically a berthing place or platform, made from concrete, stone, or metal and lying alongside, or projecting into water, made for loading and unloading ships.

The proper way to pronounce the word, "quay" is "KEE", although I have heard it pronounced "Koo-way" back in the United States, but this is clearly wrong, and it sounds silly too. I also remember one person telling me that, "It's OK for them to pronounce the word as, 'Koo-way', because language evolves..." This made no sense to me, and it's probably more about covering up their ignorance of how to pronounce the word correctly and butchering the language.

A quay in Minnesota would be a landing place, jetty, marina, or slipway. In Minnesota the word "marina" is by far the most common word we would use, and the quayside would be the quay itself, and the area surrounding it.

THE QUAYSIDE, POLPERRO, CORNWALL, ENGLAND

Finally, in the nautical section, I'm going to both reveal and explain one of the most common British misconceptions, which just happens to have a nautical twist built in.

The Union Jack. When people call the British flag the Union Jack, they're actually calling the flag by a nickname, and not it's actual name. This fact is virtually unknown to Americans, and to people of many other nations including many British people.

The name "Union Jack" is actually only a naval term, and the correct name for the flag of the United Kingdom, is

144

the "Union Flag". Naturally, the "Union" refers to the union between Scotland and England in 1707.

It became known as the Union Jack when it was flown at the front of all British warships, on what is called in the Navy, the Jack-staff. Hence the name "Union Jack" came into being, and it stuck.

It could technically be argued that the British flag should only be called a Union Jack, when it is flown on the Jack Staff (the most forward flag staff) on a British Warship, and at all other times it should be called a Union Flag.

Chapter 16: Football

Football. In the United States we call football, soccer, because, even though it makes no sense, we already use the word "football" as a contraction of, American Football, even though it is a game that rarely involves a foot making any sort of contact with a ball.

The word "soccer" first appeared around 1800 as an abbreviation, or rather acronym, for Association Football. To make matters easier, in 1863 the Football Association adopted the name, Association Football, to differentiate between Football and Rugby. Why did we Americans hijack the word "football" then? Simply because it was easier to say than, National Football League, or American Football.

Football, as in the original game where the foot is in almost exclusive contact with the ball throughout the entire game, is hugely popular in Britain, and throughout the rest of the world. Let me put this into stark comparison for you. Yes, NFL is huge, it's a big deal by any standards, with viewership in the region of 400 million people. These are mostly in the United States and Canada, but comparatively few in Asia, Europe, and Britain.

On the other hand, there is football. I was stunned to find that this has a viewership in the region of 3.5 BILLION people world-wide! That's 3.1 Billion more people than American Football, and with 3.1 BILLION more people who also typically call it football, and not soccer.

As a footnote on viewing figures/supporters, I always used to think that baseball was huge, and indeed it is, with about 500 million viewers. However, I was stunned yet again when I discovered that cricket positively dwarf's baseball, because cricket has viewers in the region of 2.5 billion people! Also, at about 1 billion people, even tennis has double the viewership of baseball. I can now understand why the big international money, and sponsorship, is in those games, and not in NFL and baseball, and why they're hard to compete with.

My husband has worked extensively in broadcast TV for many years, and he told me an interesting anecdote about why American Football is hugely popular with TV broadcasters in the United States. He believes it is all down to maximising opportunities for commercial advertising during a game, and he's probably right. Brian pointed out that during an American Football game, there are a few  seconds of explosive action, followed by a longer period of rest while they set up for the next play. This constant process of short-burst play, allows for a huge number of TV commercial advertising spots to be incorporated into each game. Whereas with football, AKA, soccer (the game that you play with your feet and a ball) there are far fewer opportunities to do this. This is because each half of the game runs constantly for 45 minutes before there's a break. The only other breaks in play are when someone is injured, or when the ball goes momentarily out of play. This makes perfect sense now that he explained it to me, and I think that U.S.

TV broadcasters will begin to push world football more once they find ways to incorporate more advertising slots into the game. It's all down to money.

Football is literally an obsession to many people here in Britain. Now that I'm living in Manchester, which is a city with two of the most famous football teams on the planet, I'm still deciding which one I should be rooting for, either Manchester City, or Manchester United.

The main problem here is that my husband and I don't really follow the game of football, instead, we both prefer watching either rugby, or American Football. In Fact, even though my husband is a Brit, he's watched many more games of American Football than he has world football, and he probably has better knowledge of the rules of American Football too.

American Football evolved from both Association Football and Rugby Football. Since this is part of the history of American Football, in case you weren't aware, rugby, AKA rugger, is named after Rugby School, in Rugby, England, where in the 1803's running with the ball during a regular game of football became common. Shortly after that, Rugby School football became widely popular throughout Britain in the 1850s, and 1860s. In 1871, English clubs then met to form the Rugby Football Union, or RFU. In 1892, charges of professionalism, or playing for money, were made against some clubs because they paid players for the work they missed during a game. As a result, the Northern Rugby Football Union, NU, was formed, which eventually led to the separation of clubs into either the "Rugby League" or "Rugby Union".

The development of American football involved several major divergences from both Association Football and Rugby Football. These were the rule changes instituted by Walter Camp, a Yale University graduate who is considered by many to be the "Father of American Football". His rules introduced the line of scrimmage, of down-and-distance rules, and of the legalization of blocking. The modern era of American Football really began after the 1932 National Football League playoff game, which was the first American Football game to feature hash marks, forward passes anywhere behind the line of scrimmage, and the movement of the goal posts back to the goal line. Shortly after that came the changes to the ball, by tapering off the ends in 1934, which made it appear more like a rugby ball.

During the time we were both researching and writing most of this book, in 2017/2018, the Minnesota Vikings American Football team had a great season, and almost reached the Super Bowl. For those who don't know, the Super Bowl is the ultimate prize of American Football, just as the World Cup is the ultimate prize for world football. The "Minneapolis Miracle" happened during the National Football Conference divisional play-off game on January 14th, 2018. The Minnesota Vikings were playing the New Orleans Saints, and with 10 seconds left in the game Case Kennum threw a 61-yard touchdown pass to Stefon Diggs and led to the Vikings winning by 29 to 24. It was very exciting for all of us Minnesotans. Unfortunately, the Minnesota Vikings then lost the next game to the Philadelphia Eagles, who went on to win the coveted grand prize of the season.

Even though Minnesota was not in the Super Bowl play off, the city of Minneapolis hosted the event. It was fabulous to see all the excitement that was taking place back in my home city while we were watching on TV in Manchester, England.

Our close friends, the Hurst family, are all lovers of American football, and despite the time difference between the two countries, they stayed up late to host a fabulous Super Bowl party in Manchester for us this year.

Draw. In the United Kingdom a football (soccer) game can end in a draw, or a tie. You'd never see that happen with an American Football game because we'd always go into to overtime until there is a winner.

Whilst on the subject of overtime, in the United Kingdom you would simply say "extra time". If it's an important game for a championship then yes, the Brits will allow some "extra time" for a shoot-out between teams to see who scores first to win the championship. However, a regular season game would never go into "extra time", and they often just end in a draw.

Club vs. Franchise. Association Football refer to their teams as a Club. In the United States, American Football teams would be referred to as a franchise.

Pitch. The Brits call the field a pitch, because they would assume a field is a place that a farmer would own, and it's where horses and sheep roam. There again, across

the Atlantic and back in the good old United States, if you refer to a "pitch", then we would think you are referring to pitching a ball or pitching a tent.

Kit. In Association Football, the uniform they wear is called a "kit". The "kit" includes a minimum of what should be worn and prohibits anything dangerous.

Boots vs. Cleats. If you refer to boots in the United States, then we would think you are referring to something you wear in the winter outside to keep your feet warm in below zero weather. In respect of Association Football in the United Kingdom, they are referring to the studded boots, AKA, cleats, they wear on the pitch, AKA field, while playing the game. It's basically a shoe that has studs on the bottom to make it easier to grip.

Chapter 17: Terms of Endearment

As an American in Britain, you'll frequently hear some highly unusual terms of endearment being casually used, even among strangers. It often comes as a big surprise to many visitors from the United States when someone such as a taxi driver, or news vendor, calls you either "dear", "love", "pet", or whatever is the favoured regional term according to where you are visiting.

If someone in Britain calls you "love" when they say something like, "Thanks love…" as they hand you your change for a transaction, it doesn't mean they love you, they're just trying to be nice. The word is used just like the British frequently use the term "mate". When it's used as a term of endearment, the word "love" is often written as either "luv", or "luvvie".

Men aren't immune to becoming the recipient of this word, because in Yorkshire, the word "love" is used as a friendly term between all sexes, and a man would think nothing of saying "Thanks love" to another man.

Don't be offended by this, or any other British term of endearment because it's not the Brits being sexist, or anything like that, it's just normal friendliness here. So, leave your social warrior prejudices at home and either accept it, or catch the next flight home.

Here are some of the other common terms of endearment you're most likely to either hear, or encounter during a visit to Britain.

- Sweetheart
- Boyo (usually in Wales)
- Petal
- Dearie
- Dear
- Hen (usually in reference to a female in Scotland)
- Flower
- Darling, or darlin'
- Chick
- Bruv, or Brother
- Babe
- Chuck, or Chuckie
- Pet
- Duck or duckkie (usually in, and around Stoke on Trent area in the Midlands)
- Princess (usually a Cockney term)
- My beauty
- Mi' booty (typically in Devon and Cornwall)
- Mate
- Son
- Guv or guvnor (usually in, an around London)
- Buggerlugs
- Honey bunny
- Sweetie pie
- Love
- Luvvie
- Luvvie-darling (typically amongst theatricals)

Chapter 18: Bloody Hell! and Oddities

Since it's not uncommon to hear even upper class British people use the occasional swear word, I thought that I'd include some of the curious British profanities, and other oddities in this section which includes miscellaneous items which seemed to fit into the same category.

Bloody Hell. "Bloody Hell", or just using the word "bloody," used to be considered an obscene explicative until the latter part of the 20th century. Today, it's very common to hear people use the word "bloody" as an intensifier of both the good and the bad. However, the phrase "bloody hell", is almost always used to express degrees of anger, and the degrees vary according to the inflection used in the way that it is said.

My close friend Suzy de Rooy, is also a fellow American married to a Brit, told me about her own embarrassing experience with the expression "bloody hell". Years ago, when she first met her soon to be mother-in-law, she used the term "bloody hell", thinking that she will incorporate an ordinary British term into her vocabulary. When she did, her fiancé's mother looked at her with disgust. What Suzy didn't realize was, the expression "bloody hell" was just as bad as if she would have use the "F" word. Of course, Suzy felt badly about this, but the couple still got married and can laugh about it years later.

The even worse word, "f**k" is commonly used in a wide range of expressions in Britain. However, my advice would be to avoid using it at all costs if you're trying to make a good impression. That is of course unless a lot of people are using it in the same social gathering, because in that case it would appear as if it's being accepted there. Even then, I'd still caution you to limit any use of crude/rude words, no matter how tempting this might be, especially when you're in the company of mostly strangers.

Pissed. The word "pissed" in Britain doesn't necessarily mean that you're angry, because being "pissed" commonly means that you are simply drunk.

Pissed off/Piss Off. This phrase has nothing to do with drinking or your state of sobriety, instead, it's an expression of how you feel. To be "pissed off" would mean that you're feeling upset, sad, or depressed, depending upon the circumstances. However, to tell somebody to "piss off", would be a very impolite way of saying "go away", which can often make the term confusing for Americans.

Pissed Again. This is a common expression a Brit might use if they clumsily trip on something, and stumble, when one is completely sober. They would say something like, "Oops, pissed again...." as if to make a funny reference to the fact that they're being so clumsy and incompetent at something so basic, that they may as well be attempting it in a state of complete drunkenness.

Taking the Piss. To be "taking the piss" is very different again, and is an expression meaning that you're, teasing, or even being completely unreasonable with someone. Other similar phrases would be, "taking the mickey" and "taking the Michael" which both also mean that you are gently making fun of or teasing someone.

Bugger. This one is a real British curiosity because the obvious face value meaning of the word usually has absolutely nothing to do with how it's used, and the way it's said. For most people, the word "bugger" is an almost classless way of expressing mild annoyance with something. For example, if you dropped and broke a plate you would often hear a Brit exclaim, "Aww, bugger!"

Bugger off. The Brits would use the term "bugger off" as a sort of mild to medium level way of telling someone to go away. However, depending upon the inflection in the voice, it can also be used in a fun way between friends. I'd never heard this phrase before I visited Cornwall for the first time, and we found out that the proprietor of our favourite hotel is known locally as "Bugger-off Bill!" Obviously, it is because he uses the phrase rather often, and now that we've stayed with them, many times, I've often heard him use the phrase when we've all been chatting socially. We totally understand him and why he uses the phrase too, and we typically agree with his sentiments under the circumstances.

Get Stuffed. Depending on how forceful you use this phrase and the inflection in our voice, "get stuffed" can mean to mildly "go away", or it can also mean, "go f**k yourself!"

Obscene Gestures. Instead of sticking up your middle finger like we Americans do if we want to make an obscene gesture, the British do this with an inverted Churchill-style "V-Sign". This is accomplished by sticking up your first two fingers, however, the palm of your hand must always be facing inwards towards yourself. By turning your palm outwards towards the other person, you're displaying Winston Churchill's world-famous "V" for victory sign.

I decided to research why the "V" sign with the back of the hand facing outwards is an insulting gesture and found it a very interesting journey. Although no one could ever say for certain, it seems most probable that it comes from the time around the Battle of Agincourt, in 1415. At that time in history, the English Longbow was the most feared weapon a soldier could carry on the battlefield. This was a mighty weapon, which required great finger, hand, arm, and upper back strength to draw and fire. If the French ever captured an English bowman, apparently, they would chop off his first two fingers, the same fingers he used to draw the Longbow with. As the English soldiers assumed their battle lines, the bowmen taunted the French with the "V" sign insult, to show that we have our two bow fingers, and we're going to use them against you. The result was that the English army beat the French army, and perhaps the insulting gestures helped in the process of winning one of the most important battles in the 100-years' war.

Mate. The word "mate" is commonly used by Brits as an informal term for a friend. The reason for this is a little unclear, although there are several interesting thoughts as to why this is. For example, one theory has it that it's from the late Middle-English (circa the 14th century) word for both, meat, and comrade, and therefore, meant people who were friendly enough to share food together.

Another alternate explanation is that it comes from the fact that Britain is a great seafaring nation, with a long naval history. The word "matelot" meaning a sailor, seaman, mariner or seafarer, and the word "mate" meaning boon companion, could be part of why it has gradually crept into common use by the Brits.

Perhaps it's a combination of the two, and more I've not covered. No one really knows for certain, but whatever the origins were as to why the Brits use the word, at least you know to expect to hear it when you visit Britain.

You may even hear British people that often don't even know each other use the word, such as when passing someone in a pub, and making the acknowledgement, "Alright mate…" This isn't a question that begs an answer, although occasionally you might hear a reply such as, "Aye" or "Yes", accompanied by a nodding of heads. This use of the word "mate" is almost always nothing more than an informal friendly acknowledgement.

Bob's your uncle. Brits would say "Bob's your uncle" as an expression meaning that everything will be fine. It originated in 1887 when the British Prime Minister of the time, Robert Gascoyne-Cecil, appointed his nephew,

Arthur James Balfour, to be the Minister for Ireland. Arthur made a reference to the Prime Minister as "Uncle Bob" and the phrase has been used ever since. It's very easy to become a government Minister when Bob's your uncle!

Knocked up. We were once at a party in Manchester with people from the British Actors Equity Union, and I was chatting with a lovely gal who told me about some of her experiences in the United States. Apparently, when she visited Virginia several years before, she had asked the hotel concierge if someone could "knock her up" in the morning at a certain time. Little did she know that in the United States, the term "getting knocked up" doesn't mean that someone will politely knock on your  door to wake you as an alarm call at a specific time. Instead, her intended wake-up call has a very different meaning, because in America it means that you have been made pregnant! Therefore, in American-speak, she was effectively asking the hotel clerk to make her pregnant at a specific time the next morning, when in reality she had only asked for a wake-up call.

In Britain, the phrase "to be knocked up" comes from the time of the industrial revolution, in the 19th and early 20th centuries. In those days, people who either didn't own, or couldn't afford an alarm clock, and yet who still needed to get up at a certain time to start work at the local factory, employed the services of the local "knocker-upper". This was a person, usually a man, who would be paid by each household to tap on the bedroom window of each client using a very long stick until the person was awake and acknowledged as such. I asked my husband Brian about this, and he clearly remembers stories being told to him by his grandmother and her sisters, about the local "knocker-upper" and what he used to charge etc.

While I'm vaguely on the subject of being pregnant, in Britain, they would call a stroller/pushchair, a pram. This is from the shortening of the word, perambulator, which is a noun meaning, "A small vehicle with four wheels in which a baby or child is pushed around". I did know this one thanks to the children's book by Jean de Brunhoff, "The Story of Babar, the Little Elephant".

Knee's up. A "knee's up" in Britain, means a very informal gathering and party, or virtually any type of high-energy celebration. A genuine old-fashioned "knees up" would involve lots of impromptu dancing, drinking, and even singing.

The phrase is almost certainly Cockney in origin, and in the 19th and early to mid-20th centuries the impromptu party with friends would have typically centred around a piano in the local pub, or in someone's home. Today, the

160

local pub and piano are no longer the typical focal point of the gathering, but the phrase is still commonly used.

Chin Wag. A "chin wag" is basically a British way of saying, to have a gossip or chat about something, someone, or just about life in general. For example, I might say to my husband that,

"I am going over to Suzy's for a good old chin wag."

Aerial. In Britain, an aerial what we in America would call a TV or radio antenna.

A Cock-up. A Brit would use this term if something had gone badly wrong and things were a mess, for either themselves, or a third party.

It's generally assumed to have a vulgar meaning, but it hasn't. instead it originates from a poem by Robert Burns called, "Cock-up your beaver". I implore everyone to now refocus their mind from the gutter, and back onto the fact that he was actually merely referring to adorning a beaver fur hat by putting a cock's feather into it.

"Cock", in this sense means to "turn up at the edge at a jaunty angle", or "stand up conspicuously". In the 16 and 1700's it has been recorded that people would "cock-up" their eyes, nose, hats, bonnets and to "cock a snook".

Today in Britain, the phrase "cock-up" refers to a complete mess, stupid organisation, or ridiculous design etc. As an example, "That was a real cock-up when someone on the German submarine U-1206 in World War 2, flushed the toilet while submerged and nearly sunk the ship, causing it to surface in an emergency right in front of the British who then sank it!"

Chuffed. When a Brit is "chuffed" about something, this means that they are exceptionally pleased, proud, or happy about something. For example, "I'm chuffed to bits about my son's promotion!"

Fancy. The Brits don't merely use the word "fancy" to describe something which is ornate, it has other meanings too. They often use the word "fancy" as a way of expressing their like, or desire of something, or someone. For example, "I fancy a glass of prosecco this evening."

Cheeky. When a Brit is being "cheeky" they are teasing or making fun of someone or something, usually in a nice way. My husband, Brian, is almost always "guilty as charged" in this respect, and

BRIAN BEING "CHEEKY" ON OUR HONEYMOON IN POLPERRO, ENGLAND

sometimes I think that he should have been given the word "cheeky" as his middle name!

162

Punt. In America, the word "punt" is solely associated with American Football when the ball is cleared right down the field. However, in Britain, the word has several different meanings.

In British and world football, this would probably be called a drop kick. A punt in rugby is a kick which connects with the ball before it touches the ground. A punt is also slang for a bet, or a gamble, and someone might say, "I took a punt on a horse in the 3.30 race." Lastly, a punt is also a term for a flat-bottomed shallow water river boat with a square bow. It uses a long pole for propulsion, which is used to push the boat along the river bed, and this action is called punting.

Bollocks. No, they're not directly referring to testicles when they use the word. Instead, when using the word "bollocks" the Brits are saying something is nonsense, rubbish, of poor quality, there's been a misfortune, or about saying something stupid. I talk about the British use of the word "rubbish" in another section.

"Bollocks" is a Middle English word dating back to the 13th century which does mean "testicles". Conversely, the word is also used in idiomatic phrases about something which is admired or approved of. In this case, a Brit would say something like "It's the dog's bollocks" or simply "The bollocks" when referring to something.

Hockey. "Hockey" in Britain always refers to field hockey, and not ice hockey, as would be the American, or Canadian common use of the word.

Knackered. The British would sometimes use the word "knackered" if they were tired, or exhausted. It is also used when referring to something that is broken and needs fixing or replacing. For example, "It looks like we need a new TV, our old one is knackered."

To ring. In Britain, to ring someone, or give someone a ring, is to call them on the phone, and not to get engaged to them or make them an extravagant gift. For example, "I'll ring you later."

Schedule. This one always makes laugh when Brian says he will check his "Shed-yul", whereas in the United States we would say "Sked-yul". He sounds so posh to me when he says "shed-yul".

Posh. Since I've just mentioned the word "posh" I may as well explain what it means, and its origin. Posh, means luxurious, upper class, snooty, classy, and expensive, and was first recorded in 1914.

The word apparently came into use via the Peninsular and Oriental Steam Navigation Company, or P&O line, which between 1842 to 1970 carried passengers and mail between England and India. On the journey from England to India, the best cabins which were coolest and with the views of land for the entire journey were on the Port side of the ship on the Outward part, and on the return journey they were on the Starboard Home. This is why the acronym, P.O.S.H. was stamped onto the tickets of passengers with those cabins. It meant that they were the very best cabins, and the most expensive tickets.

Bird. In Britain, if a man refers to a "bird", then he's almost certainly referring to an attractive young woman.

For example, a couple of guys might be walking down the street, when one notices a particularly attractive woman walking in the 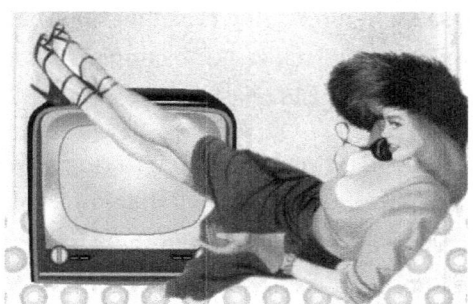 opposite direction. He would then say to his friend, "Hey, did you see that really fit looking bird over there!"

A Fit Bird. "A fit bird" refers to a good-looking shapely woman. The word "fit" being used as way of intensifying and enhancing the attractiveness of the person they're referring to thanks to their exceptionally good body shape. For example, "She's well fit!" which is Brit-speak for, "She's particularly attractive and has an exceptionally well proportioned and athletic-looking body."

Bloke. The British sometime refer to a man as a bloke, which is essentially an interchangeable term. The earliest recorded use of the word dates to the early 19th century when it was first recorded as a London slang term. The precise origin of the word is unknown and is possibly thought to be a combination of Roman, Celtic and Welsh.

Anorak. To be an "anorak" in Britain, is to be a very particular kind of geeky person, who possesses exceptional specialist knowledge of some obscure hobby such as bird watchers or train spotting.

Fag. I heard this word mentioned a lot when I first came to Britain. Here, the word "fag" refers to a cigarette.

Unfortunately, in American culture the word "faggot" is also used as a derogatory term for a homosexual person. However, in Britain, the word "faggots" refer to a traditional dish made from meat off-cuts and offal, especially pork. Faggots originated as a traditional cheap food for ordinary country people in Western England and the West Midlands in the mid-nineteenth century.

Tights. In Britain, "tights" are the equivalent of American pantyhose with two legs. "Stockings" is exclusively the term used for pantyhose that are two separate garments, and which require a suspender belt to hold them up, AKA garter belt in American-speak.

Washing-up liquid. When the Brits talk about washing-up liquid, this is the equivalent of an American talking about dish soap or dish detergent. In Britain, one of the leading brands is called Fairy Liquid, which many of my American friends on social media often find confusing.

Smart. When in Britain, you'll often hear people use the word "smart" when complimenting someone, or referring to something that is nice, good, or exceptional. For example, "You look smart today.", or "That's a smart looking car!"

Cracking. The word "cracking" would be used in Britain to express something that is fun, or joyful, or good. For example, "We're having a cracking good time writing this book!" The Wallace character in the British Claymation

TV series, Wallace and Gromit, created by Nick Park of Aardman Animations, was famous for using the word "cracking" and is almost certainly partly responsible for the current resurgence in the use and popularity of the word.

Telly. In Britain the word "telly" is referring to a television set, or TV.

Brilliant. When someone from Britain is happy about something, or they are complimenting you for something, then they might use the word "brilliant" to express themselves. For example, they might compliment your work by saying, "You did a brilliant job in decorating the lounge!" The word "brilliant" could be used to replace the greatly overused American word "Awesome".

Cheers. The word "cheers" is of course as a salute when having a drink, and to a degree it is universal in use. However, you will also hear it used a lot in Britain when you are saying either thank you, or good bye. For example, "Cheers for doing that for me mate." If someone has done you a favour, or "Cheers, see you soon.", if you're saying goodbye.

Maths. The Brits would use the word "maths" as the shortened noun for Mathematics, in the same way that an American would say, "math".

Sorted. This is something you don't hear said a lot in the United States, however, in the United Kingdom I've heard the word "sorted" used many times. For example, a Brit might say, "I'll get the paperwork sorted for you." or "We got the electrical work sorted now." Alternatively, an

American would say that it's been "taken care of" or something like that.

Dodgy. I love the word "dodgy" and think it's a fabulously descriptive word for many reasons. "Dodgy" is an adjective that means, chancy, dicey, dangerous, unsafe, crafty, cunning, or slick. If something is "dodgy" then it is of uncertain outcome and fraught with risk.

The word can be used in several ways by the Brits, so here are a few examples. "That guy over there looks a bit dodgy, we'd best avoid him." or "That shelf looks a bit dodgy, I wouldn't put anything heavy on it."

The word is amazingly flexible, and useful, and this is part of why I love it so much. The other reason is that I just enjoy saying it. The etymology of the word is a little vague, but from my research it first came into use in mid-19th century England, and is derived from the verb dodge with the letter "Y" added at the end.

Mum/Mummy. This variation on what we Americans would say took me by complete surprise. I knew the Brits referred to their mothers as either "mum" or "mummy", however, I honestly initially thought it was still spelled the way we would in the United States, as in, "mom" or "mommy". I first saw the British spelling on Christmas cards that said, "To Mum" in our local supermarket, and that was when I realised the difference. I guess you live and learn...

Plaster. In Britain, if you cut yourself then you wouldn't ask for a Band Aid, because that's an eponym brand name, instead, you'd simply ask for a "plaster", or a "sticking plaster".

Cotton Bud. Similarly, you would never ask for a Q-tip because that is also an eponym brand name, and instead you would simply ask for a "cotton bud".

Anti-clockwise. The British term would be, "anti-clockwise", while we Americans would say, "counter-clockwise".

Sod. The British and the Americans sometimes use the word "sod" about the surface of ground with grass growing on it. Another word for this would be turf.

However, the Brits use the term more frequently about someone who is annoying, rude or unpleasant, a pervert, deviant, deviate, degenerate, reprobate, miscreant, wrongdoer, offender, or overall bad person. In this respect, the word is a shortening of the word "sodomize", and the rest either is, or should be obvious!

Sod off. Now that you know how the British most commonly use the word "sod", when you tell someone to "Sod off", you're effectively saying in impolite terms to, "Go away" or "Get lost". I'm sure that you can join the dots for yourself about the sentiment behind the spoken word.

Sod's law. "Sod's law" is kind of like "Murphy's law", in that whatever can go wrong, will go wrong. "Sod's law" usually takes the sentiment even further to mean that whatever it is will always go wrong and usually have the worst possible outcome.

Plonker. The word "plonker" is an offensive British word which usually means that someone is foolish or inept. It can refer to a penis, or dick, and therefore, if you call someone a "plonker", then you're effectively calling them the same. The word was made popular in the great British comedy TV show "Only Fools and Horses" by the character "Del Boy", who often called his brother "Rodney" a "plonker!"

Quid. You will often hear people in Britain use the word "quid" when referring to a unit of currency. The word "quid" is a slang term for the British Pound Sterling and interestingly, even though it's a slang term, it is still often

used by professional forex traders to refer to millions of units of the currency.

The origin of the word "quid" is probably from the Latin word "quid" which means "something", hence the expression "quid pro quo", which means "something for something".

An example of the use of the word "quid" in the same way that a Brit would, could be like this, "Parking cost me two quid, what a rip-off!" or "Pasties have been reduced to a quid each, let's get some before they're all gone!"

Bodge. A "bodge" in Britain is makeshift solution that will probably suffice until the lasting solution can be found. Alternatively, it can also mean a poor job/repair that just about works and was done by an incompetent person.

170

Hump. If a Brit has got the "hump" it means that for some reason they're annoyed, touchy, or even combative.

Jiggery-pokery. "Jiggery-pokery" is a phrase I also love for many reasons, probably because it's so descriptive, and you can read whatever you want into it. If you're a fan of the BBC TV show "Doctor Who", then you'll have heard this term many times. When you next watch the show, keep an ear-open for the term. "Jiggery-pokery" has several meanings, for example it usually means to fiddle around with something, but it can also mean to be deceitful or dishonest, or it can mean that something naughty, usually sexual, is going on.

Kerfuffle. A "kerfuffle" is Brit-speak for a commotion, or disturbance of some sort. I clearly remember that when we were in Cornwall on Holiday for the very first time, I heard it said no less than 4 times from 4 different people within an hour or less. Yes, since I moved to this country I seem to be taking notice of the some of the most unusual conversations.

According to my research, the word "kerfuffle" originated in Scotland, with the word "fuffle" which was first used in 16th century Scottish-English as a verb meaning "to dishevel". The addition of the prefix "car" eventually changed to "ker", to complete the word "kerfuffle". The additional word "car" was probably derived from a Scottish Gaelic word meaning, "awkward" or "wrong".

Holiday. Going on holiday in Britain is not what we Americans think of as a Holiday. A holiday for people in the United States is merely the mandatory time off work at Christmas, New Year's, and Easter, etc... However, a holiday in The United Kingdom is what we  Americans would call a vacation. Whereas in Britain, a vacation means, the action of leaving something one has previously occupied, such as a house or building.

In Britain, if you work 5 days per week, then by law you are currently entitled to have a 5.6 weeks of paid holiday time each year. While I'm talking about time off work in Britain, it's currently the law to have statutory maternity leave of up to 52 weeks if you wish. However, you don't have to take the full 52 weeks off, but you must take 2 weeks leave after your baby is born, or 4 weeks if you work in a factory.

Drive-thru. In Britain, I think that you'd receive some sort of prize if you could ever find a drive-thru, or rather drive through bank, or even coffee shop such as Starbucks. These things are rarer here in Britain than a donkey that can play the piano... I'm just sayin'...

Whilst on this subject, Americans should also be prepared for smaller portions and sizes in fast food chains such as McDonalds. In Britain, a large drink is the equivalent of a medium size in the United States.

Also, Brits don't have a "take out", and instead they will have "take away" meal. It means the same thing though, and it shouldn't be hard to work that one out.

Ice. Ice in drinks is rarely seen in Britain, and cold drinks can be a rarity too. My husband tells me that it's because the ice will soon melt and dilute the drink, therefore, the thought of drinking diluted cola isn't very appealing. They also automatically add a slice of lemon in your cola which can be annoying if you don't like it.

He also tells me that many British beers are designed to be served at room temperature, because this allows the true flavour of the beer to come through. I don't know for certain if he's right or not, but I do know that lack of being served ice automatically in a drink is quite annoying at times for me as an American.

Rules for eating with the Guest. The rule of thumb for eating food with guests is as follows. If your food is served warm, then you may start eating right away. If it is served cold, then you must wait until everyone else is served. However, if you are lucky enough to be in the presence of the Queen, then you must wait until everyone is served and the Queen always leads the way.

The Brits always use the fork and a knife, and technically it's disrespectful to use a fork alone. If you know any Americans in Britain, or if you're American, then you'll already have noticed that we Americans always tend eat with just our fork.

This American habit seems to have a point of origin that even many Americans aren't aware of. At the time of the revolutionary war, those who were the revolutionaries frequenting the taverns and eating houses could be easily identified by this secret method of eating their food. In eating this way, it was possible to identify your companions while the colonies were still under British rule.

Weather. The weather is always a good topic of conversation in Britain, and at times one might think that it's a national pastime. It's always a safe bet to use the weather as the topic, especially if you wish to strike up a conversation with a complete stranger.

You should also be prepared for some very changeable weather in Britain, therefore, it's always a good idea to carry a folding umbrella and one of those folding stow-away plastic rain coats. The best time to visit Britain to get the best weather would usually be in May and June.

To-Go Box? It's not common in Britain to ask for a "to-go box" because the portions here are generally much smaller than in America. If ever you do ask for one, then be prepared to receive your food crudely wrapped in makeshift tin foil or something similar. A "to-go box" here is also often called a "doggy bag". I remember growing up in the 70's in Minnesota when the term "doggy bag" was used, but it seems to have disappeared from use in recent years.

A Skip. A "skip" in Britain, is what we in America would call a dumpster. In Britain, a "skip" is a large open-topped container designed for waste, usually used by builders, and which is then loaded onto a special type of lorry, AKA truck. A "skip" isn't emptied directly into landfill or recycling, instead it is removed from the truck and replaced by an empty "skip" so the truck can deliver that to another location.

Many people in Britain don't even know why a "skip" has that name, so I'll explain. The word "skip" comes from the Old English word "sceppe" which itself comes from the old Norse word "skeepa", and both words mean, basket. This word probably came to Britain, between 600AD and the year 1066 when William the Conqueror and his army became the last to invade Britain.

I'm Sorry. For some reason, the Brits tend to apologise a lot. We've occasionally stopped people and asked for directions, and if they don't know, they still apologise and say that they are sorry.

Coming from Minnesota I didn't even really notice at first, because part of being "Minnesota Nice" also means that you end up apologizing a lot. In that respect, we're very much like the British. I've occasionally heard

Minnesota people say, "Ope, sorry" rather often, such as if you have accidently bumped into someone.

When this was first pointed out to me, my first thoughts were. "No, I don't do anything like that!" Then, sure enough I was in our local supermarket shortly  afterward, I turned a blind corner in an aisle and almost ran into someone. Without even thinking, I immediately said, "Ope, sorry!" At that point I literally cringed to myself on the inside, and I realized that I am, and will always be, 100% Minnesotan. By apologising a lot like the Brits do, I'll probably fit-in just fine here in this country. I honestly don't think that the Brits apologise any more than we do in Minnesota, and I prefer to believe that we're all just polite and respectful people in general.

Keen. For some reason, the word "keen" makes me laugh every time I hear my husband say it. "Keen" is a word which is often used by Brits when they are eager about something. For example, "I'm keen to get this book published." Which is true, because this is very different to all other books we've published to date, and it's been the most enjoyable to research and write.

Engaged. When a phone is "engaged" in Britain, it is the equivalent of the phoneline being "busy" in the United States.

Date Format. In Britain they typically write the date following the Day, Month and Year convention, whereas in the United States we use the Month, Day, Year format.

Mobile phone. A "mobile phone" in Britain is what we Americans would call a "cell phone", but unless you're completely linear, you'd have probably worked that one out easily enough. It's very important to remember that you cannot use a cell phone while you're driving a car in Britain.

Tax Included. In Britain, their version of sales tax is called VAT, which stands for Value Added Tax, and this is currently set at 20%. More importantly, when you see a price for something in a store in Britain, the sales tax, AKA the VAT, is already included, so the price you see, is always the price you pay.

TV Licence. Even if you simply own a TV set in Britain, then you must pay a licence fee, AKA a tax, for it each year. Currently, this costs £145.50, or at today's exchange rate as I write this, $205.68 USD.

At first, this sounded a little harsh, but that was before I learned what you got for it in return. This low yearly fee means that you get all 7 BBC channels WITHOUT any commercial advertising in them! You also get all the BBC radio channels, again without all the annoying adverts

177

you'd get in America! I could hardly believe it when I first saw the BBC TV channels in Britain, because being American, I've been conditioned to expect annoying TV commercials to pop up every few seconds.

Any British person who doesn't think that the EBC offers EXCELLENT value for the money they pay in a licence fee, should try living in the United States for a while. We literally must SUFFER through the painful and repetitive commercial advertising during every programme. Yes, I even spelt (AKA spelled) the word "programme" the British way.

Now that I've experienced the advert-free BBC TV channels, I've been spoilt (AKA spoiled), and now I find it challenging and annoying to watch the rubbish-packed commercial advertising TV we have in America.

Gherkins or Pickles? In Britain, they would cal an American pickle, a gherkin. This is probably because they have pickle, or piccalilli as a relish which is bought in jars here. This is a selection of chopped vegetables, and hot spice mixture in a mild mustard sauce. This dates back to around 1758 when "Paco-Lilla", or "India Pickle" was popular. It's delicious, so I suggest that you try it when you're in Britain.

Free Healthcare. In Britain, the AMAZING National Health Service provides all people who are legally allowed to live in the country, completely free health care! This is a huge difference to the United States, where you'd literally be left dying in the street if you can't afford to pay medical bills. I know this to be true, because I've seen it happen.

There are many arguments for and against a completely free system, but the fact is that, love it or hate it, and even though it occasionally has faults, the British National Health Service works amazingly well.

In my humble opinion, if anyone complains about the British National Health Service for not being as efficient as it could be, I'll put it this way. In comparison to what we have back in the United States, it's like complaining that your Rolls Royce is running a little on the rough side. This is because the British National Health System is a premier "Rolls Royce" standard health system, and I only wished that more people would realise that and treasure it.

Acclimatised and Acclimated. This was an interesting comparison of two words which mean the same thing. Naturally, if you're British you'd say that you were becoming acclimatised to something, and if you're American, then you'd say that you were becoming acclimated. The word "acclimate" comes from the French word "acclimater" which dates back to about 1792. Alternatively, the word the Brits use "acclimatise" which wasn't first attested until about 1836. This is one of the rare instances where Americans use a word that is older in recorded origin than the word the British use.

Garden, Yard, Lawn. In Britain, a garden is usually at the front, and/or rear of your house, whereas in the United States, it would be either the front lawn, or the back yard. In Britain, a back yard usually refers to a small paved area behind a 19th century style terraced house. In America, when referring to a garden, it would be a specific area of your lawn to grow vegetables.

Fringe and Bangs. If you're an American who is talking about their "bangs", then they aren't being rude, and they also aren't talking about a series of loud noises, because they would be referring to what the British would call, the fringe of their hair.

The word "bangs" in relation to the fringe of hair on your forehead, originated in the stables of horses. When a horse's tail is cut evenly in a horizontal way at a certain length, then this is called a "bangtail". Some even suggest that this term originated in Scotland, but I've not been able to substantiate that.

The "bangtail" style of hair was first used on people between 1844, with the term "bang" first being used in about 1878. Therefore, the American use of the word "bang", means either "abrupt or sudden" cut off, when referring to the style of haircut.

Washing Machines. In the United States, it's almost unknown for people to keep their washing machines and dryers in the kitchen because they're almost always in a dedicated utility room. However, in Britain, due to the homes being much smaller in general than those in the United States, the washer and dryer are commonly found in the kitchen, where they're built into the fitted units.

Rain that Wets You... In Britain, you'll often see an American scratching their head in confusion when a Brit talks about "The rain that wets you."

At first, I thought that this was just one of those British nonsense sayings that made no real sense, because all rain will wet you – right? However, after a little research, I now understand what the Brits are saying.

Naturally, all rain will make you wet, but the larger sized rain drops are usually much more spread out, than the finer drops in misty rain. This is the fine rain which the Brits refer to when they say, "The rain that wets you." The misty type of densely packed rain has a great many more drops per cubic inch than other types of rain. Therefore, the fine, misty rain, AKA "The rain that wets you.", will make you wetter more quickly than other types of less dense rain.

Touch Wood and Knock on Wood. The British will say, touch wood, and the Americans will say, knock on wood, and both mean the same thing. This is to avoid "tempting fate" and is usually performed after making a confident declaration about a situation beyond one's direct control.

The origin of this custom possibly originates in mediaeval Germany, when supernatural beings were thought to live in trees, and could be invoked for protection as needed. However, many other countries and cultures share similar beliefs in elemental beings and spirits, and other research suggested that this superstition could even be Druidic in origin, dating back some 5,000 years in Britain.

The only difference between the way the Brits and Americans might do it, is in that it's common for a British person to touch their head either instead of, or in the absence of wood. This is a self-deprecating British way of suggesting that their head is made of wood.

A.C. and Air-conditioning. In Britain, the American term, A.C. is known as "aircon". It's not common for most homes, and buildings in Britain to have air-conditioning installed, and there are precious few ceiling fans as well.

Collar and Cuffs Match. To use the phrase "collar and cuffs match" would be when you are referring to a woman who has very obviously died her hair, and the onlooker is wondering in a joking way, if the colour of her pubic hair matches the hair on her head. It's a fun way of saying that the hair colour she now has is very obviously not natural.

Fur Coat and no Knickers. To say that someone is all "fur coat and no knickers" refers to a person that appears to be wealthy, high class, and sophisticated, however, in reality, they have no substance behind them at all. A good example of this would be someone with a good

wardrobe, and a high-end car, which is usually heavily financed, and yet they can only afford to live in a shabby rented apartment in a bad area of town. This would be someone who is said to be, "fur coat and no knickers" –

all the external trappings of substance and wealth, with no real substance underneath to back-up the image.

Chav. A "chav" is a derogatory word about a type, or class of person that is always dressed in the latest designer clothes. These are either genuine brands, or more typically they are fake. A "chav" almost always brings with them uncouth, ill mannered, loud and obnoxious behaviour.

Lodgers. A "lodger" is a British term for what we'd call a "renter" in the United States.

Solicitor – Lawyer. In Britain, you'll rarely see a sign advertising a lawyer, and instead you'll see lots of offices where solicitors practice. The two are essentially the same thing in most cases, although there can be differences depending upon your legal representative in each country. In a nutshell, a solicitor is a legal practitioner who traditionally deals with most of the legal matters. The legal profession in Britain is split between solicitors and barristers, with the latter being called advocates in some countries. A barrister is a specialist lawyer. A lawyer is a person who practices law either as, an advocate, barrister, attorney, or counsellor. Even though lawyers typically hold only one title, occasionally they will hold more than one. In the United States, people commonly refer to a "solicitor" as being someone who makes cold sales calls in person, or it's someone who solicits prostitutes.

Realtor – Estate Agent. In Britain, it will be rare to find a realtor, or real estate agent, and instead you'll find plenty of estate agents. The two are basically the same thing, but there are some important differences.

In the United States, a realtor will usually handle the entire process of both advertising, negotiating, selling, arranging a mortgage if necessary, together with the conveyancing, or the preparation of all legal documents for the transferring ownership of a property.

In Britain, an estate agent will usually be engaged to advertise, negotiate and sell a property. They may also arrange an introduction to a mortgage lender, but they won't handle any of the legal paperwork related to any of that. Once a sale has been agreed, then a solicitor must be engaged to handle all the legal paperwork required for the conveyancing, and any mortgage that might be needed.

Grafting. You'll frequently hear Brits use the term "graft" or "grafting" in relation to exceptionally hard work. The word "graft" is based on the phrase "spade's graft", which meant the amount of earth that one stroke of a spade will move. This is itself based on the Old Norse word "grǫftr", which means "digging".

The term "grafting" in relation to meaning hard work, originated around the time of the Norman Conquest of Britain in 1066. Immediately after the Battle of Hastings was won, the Norman invaders hastily constructed makeshift fortifications to help them subdue the indigenous population.

To help them do this, the Norman invaders used the native Anglo-Saxons as forced labour to build these fortifications and dig the moats around them. Apparently, moat digging and excavating the foundations needed for castles was the hardest work of all. Hence the term, to "graft", or "grafting", to signify this work came into common use, and from that time onwards, it stuck.

184

Barking mad. The Brits frequently use the term "barking mad", or more commonly the shortened term "barking", when referring to someone who is crazy, or something that doesn't make any sense. For example, someone might say, "That woman is nice enough to chat with, but she's totally barking…" meaning that she's a nice person, but a little odd, unusual, or eccentric.

The district of Barking in London is sometimes cited as being the origin of the phrase because of the alleged existence of a mediaeval insane asylum attached to Barking Abbey. The phrase first appeared around the mid-20th century, but a much more likely origin is in comparing an insane person to a mad dog barking for no reason.

Fizzog. The British occasionally use the term "fizzog" for a person's face in Britain, and it's usually used in a slightly derogatory way, but not always.

The word "fizzog" is slang taken from the word "physiognomy". This is the assessment of character, and/or their personality from a person's outer appearance, and in particular, their face. The word can trace its origins back to the Anglo-Norman period, but it's original source is from the Latin word "physiognomic", and before that, an Ancient Greek word meaning "the science or art of judging a man by his features".

Rubbish. Rubbish in Britain is what you call the garbage, or trash, in the United States. You can also use the word, Rubbish, if you think something is bad, useless or not right. For example, "The service we received at that restaurant was absolutely rubbish!"

Bin. The garbage, or wastebasket, in the United States is called a can, whereas in Britain it would be called a waste bin, or rubbish bin. The large garbage cans we Americans would have outside our homes would be called a dustbin in Britain. This is a throw-back to the days of open coal fires and when the bins were made of metal so that they could handle dumping hot coals and dust from the ashes of the fire right into them.

Tea Towel. A Tea Towel is the British way to say dish towel. They are very popular in Britain, and you can get all sorts of varieties of them at the tourist shops dotted around resorts and places of public interest. You could easily buy a dish towel with the place names printed on, from all the different tourist spots you visited in Britain. Happy memories to take back home to America with you.

Nappy. A nappy in Britain, is the same as a diaper in the Unites States. However, a nap, is universal, and is still something that you do in the afternoon.

Dummy. A dummy in Britain, is a pacifier for us Americans. I've heard them called many things before, including a pacifier, binky, paci, but I'd never heard them called a "dummy" before. We Americans would use the term "dummy" when referring to a stupid person.

A to Zed. Instead of saying just A to Z, pronounced "zee" as we Americans would say it, the British and most other English-speaking countries pronounce it, A to "Zed".

"Zed" comes from the Greek word "zeta". This then turned into the Old French way of saying "zede", and around the 15th century, the English use of the word turned into "zed". I am quite shocked to find out the United States is the only place in the world that pronounces it "zee".

Post. To Post something in Britain, is to mail something in the United States. I've never heard Brian say that he needed to go to the mail box, instead, he's always used the term, post box.

He's often pointed out how confused some people are in America when he uses the term "post a letter". He's told me how people don't seem to understand what he means, unless he uses the term "mail a letter". This seems especially odd when Americans send their mail through the United States Postal Service, and not the United States Mail Service.

In addition, you won't see mail boxes at the end of driveways in Britain. Instead, houses have post boxes and postal flaps built into the door of their homes.

Weight in stones. This was a new one for me. I'd never heard of people weighing themselves by the "stone" before I came to Britain. Therefore, to clarify it for everyone else, 1 stone equals 14 pounds. Someone who weighs 17 ½ stones, will weigh 245 pounds, and someone who weighs 8 stones, will weigh 112 pounds.

The stone as a measurement of weight is an ancient system which came about through tradesmen using set weights of stones as a method of measuring quantities of goods. This was confusing because there wasn't a universal system, and different tradesmen's stones often weighed different amounts. The United Kingdom's imperial system adopted the wool stone weight of 14 pounds in 1835.

Wellies. The word "wellies" in Britain is short for Wellington boots, which we American would call rain boots, or rubber boots. To further add to the confusion, you may also find them referred to as gumboots in Britain.

Wellington boots have a long and noble history because they were invented by The Duke of Wellington who defeated Napoleon at the Battle of Waterloo in 1815. They were based upon Hessian-style boots he wore, and after the battle, they quickly became fashionable among the British aristocracy in the early 19th century.

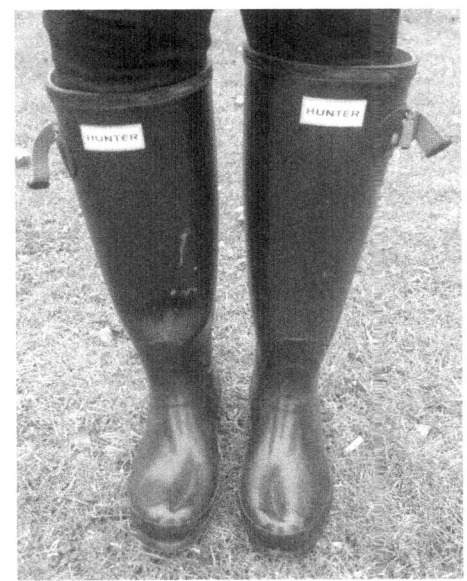

Today in Britain, Wellington boots are classless, and are common in contemporary society among farmers, hunters, outdoors enthusiasts, and even girls about town like me, who also enjoy splashing in puddles. Wellington boots are thankfully waterproof and are most often made from rubber or something similar, and generally rise to just below knee-high, although shorter Wellies can be found if you need them as part of your fashion outfit.

Brolly. This is an abbreviation for umbrella, and in Britain, it's often a good idea to always carry one with you, just in case.

Very occasionally you'll find an umbrella called a "gamp", which after Sarah, or Sairey Gamp who is a nurse in the novel "Martin Chuzzlewit" by Charles Dickens.

Rubber. Obviously, this is a type of material used in such things as tyres, AKA, tires. However, in Great Britain, they also call an "eraser", a "rubber", whereas in the United States, the word "rubber" most commonly refers to a condom. You can imagine how this slight difference in meaning might create terrible mix ups at work, and in your

private life. It's highly embarrassing if you're on a hot date that might get even hotter, and you ask for a rubber at the late night chemist shop, AKA, pharmacy, and they think you are talking about an eraser. What a passion-killer!

Aluminum/Aluminium. Aluminum is spelled the same in both the U.S. and U.K., but they also use the word Aluminium which still means the same thing which is a silver/white metal. When researching the meaning behind why there are two correct spellings for the same word, I was very surprised at where this led me.

The metal element was derived from the mineral, alumina, and the name was first proposed by the English chemist Sir Humphry Davy. This is where the confusion seems to have begun, because Davy made a complete mess of naming the new element. His first spelling in 1808 was "alumium". In 1812, he proposed the name "aluminum" when referring to the element in his book "Elements of Chemical Philosophy". Despite Davy's naming fiasco to date in 1812, eventually the official name "aluminium" was adopted to conform with the "-ium" ending of the names of most other elements

To further add to the confusion, Webster's Dictionary of 1828 enters the stage. This is because it only contains the spelling "aluminum", even though American chemists were commonly spelling the word "aluminium". In fact, this was the standard spelling of the word throughout the 19th century. The shift to the "aluminum" spelled word began in about 1890-5 onwards, and probably because it was easier to say. In 1925 the American Chemical Society eventually officially changed it back to " aluminum".

Meanwhile, back in Britain, they simply continued to use the originally accepted spelling of the word "aluminium", just as they do to this day. This is also why there are officially two correct spellings of the same word.

Flashlight and Torch. When I had finally settled into our home in Manchester, England, my new husband and I decided that we should do some small renovation work to make life a little easier for us now that there were two people living in the place. I set to painting a room, while my husband was cleaning and replacing light fittings.

He was working in the bathroom, and I was painting in the lounge, when Brian calls out to me, "Honey can you please bring a torch into the bathroom?" At this point I'm

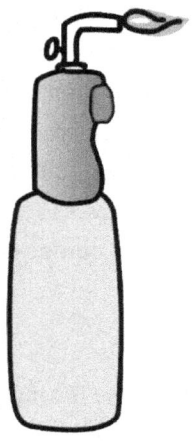 totally confused, and thinking to myself, "Do we even have a torch? Why would he want a torch in the bathroom? Does he want to set something on fire, or do some soldering plumbing work?"

This is because to me, the word "torch" was a shortening of blowtorch. I then decided to go into the bathroom and clarify what he meant. It was in darkness, and my husband was standing on the upper rung of a step ladder apparently doing something with the light fitting. I asked him questioningly, "A torch?" He replies, "Yes, a torch, it's too dark and I need to see what I am doing." I laughed aloud, and said "Oh, you mean a flashlight!" He then stoically replies with a straight face and just a hint of sarcasm, "No, I don't want a flashing light, I want a steady beam of light, and that's why I asked for a torch!" I simply laughed and said, "Ok, got it, I'll be right back."

I remember chuckling to myself, leaving my bewildered husband shaking his head in disbelief that I didn't know what a torch was. It was news to me at the time, that in Britain they almost never use the term "flashlight", and instead they always call it a torch.

I then decided to find out why we Americans call a torch, a flashlight, and did some research. It seems that there is a perfectly good reason why we call them a flashlight, albeit a very outdated one. The early torches, or rather flashlights, ran on zinc-carbon batteries which could not provide a steady electric current. In fact, they were so inefficient that during use they required periodic rest before they could be used again.   The early  devices also used highly inefficient carbon-filament bulbs which didn't provide a steady beam of light. Therefore, it was the inefficient lightbulb combined with the short periods of intermittent resting during use which gave rise to the term flashlight.

It really was because the early devices tended to provide occasional extended flashes of light, rather than the consistently steady beam of light provided by the modern torch. Whereas the term "torch" originally referred to a stick with combustible material attached at one end, which is then ignited to provide a steady non-flashing light source. So basically, we were both right.

Other than that, the renovations went well. Well, except for the problem I seemed to have which is my seeming inability to hold the light steadily focussed onto the point where someone is working. I was just laughing so much that no matter how much I tried, I simply couldn't keep the beam of light focussed in the right place!

Phone Box. I am sure most people know this, but I thought to mention it just in case you haven't. In Britain, public telephones are housed inside the large red cabins on

the high street. Sadly, these iconic public call boxes are on the decline due to the widespread use of cell phones, or as the Brits would call them, the mobile phone.

Fortunately, the very nice people at British Telecom company that owns them, has had the foresight to maintain a few of these world-famous iconic red phone boxes.

They are placed at strategic places around big cities like London and Manchester for mostly tourist use – thank you British Telecom! In the United States, we would call the equivalent, a telephone booth.

Police Box. Police boxes have been used throughout the United Kingdom since the 1920's. The original boxes were solely used to call the police if they were needed, but that soon changed. The larger police telephone box was big enough to stand inside too. They were used by police officers to hold a prisoner under arrest in what was in effect, a secure mini-cell until reinforcements could come pick them up in a police wagon. They were kind of a small police station placed at strategic locations around the city.

If you're familiar with the BBC TV series "Doctor Who", then you will know precisely what a police box looks like. The one we found in London in the picture was quite small, and was only a call box, but we do know that there is a full-size "Doctor Who" style police call box which we have yet to visit. That will be one of our next adventure excursions to the capital city.

194

Flat. In Britain, an apartment within a block would therefore be called a flat. It seems to be a lot more popular in Great Britain for people to buy a flat rather than rent, and it's even possible to buy freehold flats. Whereas in the United States, most people would rent a flat rather than buy it. It would also most likely be called a "condo" and not a "flat" if you were to purchase one back in the States.

Block of Flats. In England they do not use the term, apartment building, instead, you would call the equivalent a block of flats.

To Let. Whilst vaguely on the subject of renting a flat or a house, in Britain you would never use the term "For Rent". Instead, the Brits would say "To Let" which essentially means the same thing. Be careful though, I've often mistaken the "To Let" sign at first glance and thought the sign said "Toilet". Obviously, this can be quite an embarrassing problem if one is a little desperate, usually after traveling for some time when you really need to find a loo as soon as possible!

House Keys. This has nothing to do with how to pronounce the word, or anything like that, it's more of an interesting observation really. When I first saw a set of British house keys, I was surprised to find some of them were quite bulky and old fashioned in style.

These are very common, and the reason they use this style of key is because many of the door locks are high security ones which are built into the frames of all doors. No property in Britain would be secured merely by a lock which is fixed onto the exterior facia of a door or frame, because the home insurers would never allow this. If you ever need to buy a door lock in Britain, then always buy a multi-lever insurance-approved mortice deadlock. If you don't, then you could be in breach of your insurance policy and find yourself without cover at a crucial moment when you most need it.

Ground Floor, 1ˢᵗ Floor, 2ⁿᵈ Floor... In the United Kingdom they call the main floor, the ground floor, whereas in the United States we call it the first floor.

You can see how this is confusing, especially when you get into a lift, AKA, an elevator. Here's a brief British – American comparison guide. British Ground Floor = American 1ˢᵗ Floor, British 1ˢᵗ Floor = American 2ⁿᵈ Floor, British 2ⁿᵈ Floor = American 3ʳᵈ Floor, etc.

Lift. Since I just mentioned the word, elevator, remember that the Brits call it a lift. So, if you're in a hotel or department store, then always lookout for the signs saying "Lifts" when you want to take an elevator ride.

Naf. Naf, or naff as it's sometimes spelt, is a commonly used British slang word that doesn't really have a direct American counterpart. Naf means, to be dull, unfashionable, boring, awful, drab, or hetero, and perhaps the closest American equivalent word would be "lame".

The reason that it doesn't have a direct counterpart is probably because the word "naf" is a slang word which is part of an urban secret language called "Polary" or "Polari" which is common among the gay, theatrical, circus, and the show people subculture.

Polari was widespread in London, and particularly in the theatre, from the 1940s-1960s, but suffered a decline in the 1970s and 1980s. Fortunately, it has had a slight revival since the 1990s. "Naf", and other words of Polari slang were made famous and brought into the common British vernacular through the 1960's BBC radio programme "Round the Horne with Kenneth Horne". In the show, the amazingly talented Kenneth Williams and Hugh Paddick would perform a comedy spot as the characters, "Julian and Sandy" each week. During this regular comedy slot, the two performers would frequently use a great many words from the Polari language.

It should be noted, that a fairly common British slang word for toilet is, khazi, also spelt, carsey, which is also a word from the Polari language.

Ta – Thank you. "Ta" is a very common British way of saying thank you, especially in the North and eastern parts of the country. "Ta" is pronounced as "tar" and it comes from the Danish word for thank you, which is "tak", with the letter "k" being dropped at some point in history. Many Americans, and people from other countries too, might wonder why the British often use what is essentially a Danish word to say, "thank you".

When you dig into the history of Britain, you'll soon discover why this is. The beginning of the Viking Age in Britain dates from the 8th of June 793 and lasted until about 1050. It began when the Viking raiders destroyed the abbey on the island of Lindisfarne off the northeast coast of Northumberland, in the North Eastern part of England. This began the rapid expansion of Viking-held territory, and they eventually invaded mainland Britain to occupy large parts of the country, from the Eastern seaboard, inwards to many parts of central Britain, and beyond.

There are still a huge number of words In the modern English language that are of Viking origin. The most obvious Viking word in the English language today is, Thursday, which literally means "Thor's day". Other words include, "husband" which comes from "húsbóndi" and means "hús" (house) and "bóndi" (occupier and tiller of soil.) The word "yule" is from "jol", and it might surprise many to learn that is actually a pagan winter solstice feast.

There are still many Viking-influenced place names to be found in modern Britain. Knutsford in Cheshire, where my Anglo-American friend Jane Hughes lives is one of them. The settlement of Knutsford is included in the

Domesday Book of 1086 which was commissioned by William the Conqueror after the Norman Invasion of Britain. It was called the Domesday Book because the Old English word "Dom", which means reckoning or accounting. It's a manuscript record of the "Great Survey" of much of England and parts of Wales completed in 1086.

In it is listed "Cunetesford" which literally means "Canute's ford" after the Viking king, Canute. It was to mark a safe crossing place he chose of the river Lily which flows through the village of Knutsford to this day. King Canute ruled England between 1016 and 1035. If you're observant during a visit to Britain, you'll easily be able to spot many of these Viking-influenced names.

You'll also see many Latin and Roman-influenced names, with the most obvious being the town of Pontefract in Yorkshire. The name of "Pontefract" come from the Latin which means "broken bridge". It is a word formed by combining the word "pons", meaning "bridge" and "fractus", meaning "broken".

On the other hand, Pontefract Cakes, aren't cakes. Instead they're a type of small, circular black sweet made of liquorice, originally manufactured in the Yorkshire town of Pontefract. More importantly, they're delicious!

Chapter 19: Cockney Rhyming Slang

Cockney Rhyming Slang started in the early 19th century in the East End of London. Before I even get into what Cockney Rhyming Slang is, and how it's said, I'll first describe what a "Cockney" is.

The term "Cockney" has had many different associations, with the original term being applied to all London city-dwellers.

Eventually, it was gradually restricted to only being Londoners who were born within the sound of the bells of Bow Church, AKA St Mary-le-Bow Church in the Cheapside district of London. Eventually, the term became used to refer to all those who live in London's East End, and then to all working-class Londoners in general.

Now, I'll attempt to explain Cockney Rhyming Slang. Instead of saying the word itself, which would normally be far easier, you would use two or three words, with the last word rhyming with the original word you're referring to. These are the basics of Cockney Rhyming Slang – got it yet? I didn't think so, and if it makes you feel any easier, it took me a while too.

Eventually, some of these phrases became shortened, and they'd drop the last word/s, while the last word was still implied. This would then make other non-cockney people completely confused, and totally fail to understand what you're saying on every level.

I certainly won't be able to list them all in this book, but here are plenty for you to try from those I've already heard from my husband Brian, from some of his London-born friends, and from various TV shows and movies.

Cream Crackered. To be "cream crackered" is a Cockney Rhyming Slang term for the word "knackered", which of course means that you are tired, or exhausted.

Hank Marvin. (also, Lee Marvin). This is Cockney Rhyming Slang phrase for "starving", or very hungry. Brian sometimes uses the term "Lee Marvin", because he knew a guy called Lee Marvin who had apparently been named by his parents after the famous movie actor. I think that in American terms, the equivalent word would be that you are "hangry", which is of course itself a fusion of "hungry and "angry".

Rosy Lee. "Rosy Lee" means, perhaps unsurprisingly "tea". Of course, in Britain afternoon tea is a must, so I'm quite used to it by now. I positively love having our tea-time every day.

Dog and Bone. When Brian and I first started dating, before we set out from home he would jokingly always ask me if I had remembered to bring my "dog and bone".

The first time he said this I remember stopping dead in my tracks, and looking at him in complete confusion.   I then asked what on Earth he meant, and when he explained about Cockney Rhyming, apparently, he had been referring to my cell phone.

Today, he still double checks with me, because I can be a little forgetful at times, but I now know what he means. Now he simply asks jokingly, if I have my "dog" with me before we leave the house.

Cockney Rhyming Slang	Meaning
Apples and Pears	Stairs
Bread and cheese	Sneeze
Frog and Toad	Road
Barney Rubble	Trouble
Doogie Howsers	Trousers
Tom Cruise	Booze
Bees and Honey	Money
Bubble Bath	Laugh

Gypsy's Kiss	Piss – Yes, this means that you must use the loo!
Kick and Prance	Dance
Mork and Mindy	Windy
Raspberry Tart	Fart
Tom and Dick	Sick
Pony and Trap	Crap
Mince Pies	Eyes
Plates of Meat	Feet
German Bands	Hands
Barnet Fair	Hair
Trouble and Strife	Wife
Irish Jig	Wig
Kettle and Hob	Watch – Fob Watch
Boat Race	Face
Alan Whickers	Knickers
Adam and Eve	Believe
Cream Crackered	Knackered
Battlecruiser	Boozer – Pub/Bar
Brass Tacks	Facts
Currant Bun	Sun
Daisy Roots	Boots
Butchers Hook	Look
China Plate	Mate - Friend

Loaf of Bread	Head
Skin and Blister	Sister
Whistle and Flute	Suit
Elephant's Trunk	Drunk
Dickey Dirt	Shirt
Bin Lids	Kids
Ball and Chalk	Walk

As you might imagine, the list of Cockney Rhyming Slang goes on and on and on. If you're particularly interested to learn more, then you can even buy books entirely dedicated to the subject.

No matter which side of the pond you come from, or which side you might live, give Cockney Rhyming Slang a try. Also, be sure to make up some of your own as you do so, and to try them out on your significant other. This is SO much fun, especially to see the looks of bewilderment, confusion, and tears of laughter that results from it all! Who knows, soon you may even have your own secret language that only the two of you will be able to understand.

Chapter 20: Retail Therapy

Britain has some fabulous places to shop, and the big cities such as London, Manchester, Edinburgh, Cardiff, and Birmingham have much to offer visiting tourists. London and Manchester in particular, have a thriving international fashion scene.

This shouldn't come as any surprise really, after all, London, or rather "Swinging London" was at the heart of the cultural and fashion revolution of the 1960's, and that legacy continues to this day. Back then, Mary Quant led a global fashion revolution with the introduction of the miniskirt, and ever-shorter skirts could be seen almost every day in the iconic shopping areas such as, King's Road, Kensington, Chelsea and Carnaby Street. This must have been a magical time to live through, with classic Mini-

Cooper and E-Type Jaguar sports cars frequently serving as transport for the ladies wearing those micro-mini skirts!

In Manchester today, there are many fabulous places to go shopping. It really is such a gorgeous city to walk around and explore, while at the same time enjoying some excellent retail therapy.

Since public transports is excellent in Britain in general, we love to take the bus into town to save the hassles of parking and traffic jams. Thankfully, since many city centres in Britain have been especially designed for walking, there are even days when we just walk to the city centre. It's 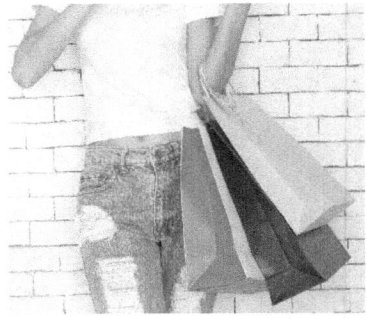 only a 3-mile journey from home, a short stretch of the legs really, and we all need to take more exercise – right?

There are three important points about shopping in Britain that you should remember. Firstly, in Britain, a shop is what we Americans would call a store. Secondly, a supermarket is what we'd call a grocery store in the United States. Thirdly, it's important to remember that when shopping in Great Britain you must bring your own shopping bag/s with you. If you don't, then be prepared to pay 5p for a reusable plastic bag. This is a huge pet peeve of Brian's and he would sooner walk home juggling ten items with his hands and feet, rather than pay the 5p for a bag. I have witnessed him doing this myself which is quite hilarious.

When I first arrived in England it's hard to know in advance which shops and department stores are the best to visit when you're searching for something specific. To make it easier for my fellow Americans who might visit Britain, and for my own family in America who are already planning visits, I've compiled a list of some of the stores you'll find here. I have also listed what type of store each might relate to back in the United States.

Asda. First off, we have Asda, which I haven't visited yet in Britain. From what I've seen of their commercials, and from what I've been told by others, it's just like Walmart, which is the parent company in the United States. This would explain why they are so similar.

Sainsbury's. This is the 2nd largest supermarket chain in the United Kingdom, with Tesco being the largest. We just seem to prefer Sainsbury's, probably because their store is close to where we live, and we can easily walk there and back. The main difference between the supermarkets here in Britain, and those in America, especially in the Midwest, is that we don't often have wide ranges of clothing and large household items such as TV's for sale at our local Cub Foods store in Minnesota. Other States and stores obviously have regional variations on this theme, and Walmart is a very different national chain.

I found it very odd that in the United Kingdom you won't find eggs stored in the refrigerated section of the supermarket. Instead, eggs are to be found in the same aisle as bread, or something similar. This still seems really

 strange to me, because we always keep eggs in refrigerated sections of stores in the United States.

Target. Just Kidding! Unfortunately, we don't have Target Stores in the United Kingdom. I love shopping at Target, and this is one of the things I miss the most about living here in Britain. My girlfriends here, and my husband, all tell me that the closest equivalent store to Target in Britain, is Tesco. Apparently, Tesco carry a very similar range of items that Target does, and the layout of the stores aren't dissimilar either. I was also told that it was the dominance of Tesco stores in Britain and Europe that prevented Target expanding into the market on this side of the pond. I don't know if this is true or not, but that would seem to make sense if it is.

Marks and Spencer. I suppose that this upmarket British store would be something in between a Target and a J.C. Penney's, or Kohl's back in America.

Primark. The best way I can compare Primark would be that they are like the Forever 21 stores in the United States. The clothing at Primark isn't expensive, and since you usually pay for what you get, it may not be of the very highest quality, but you can usually find a good item of essential clothing, or throw-away style accessories, at a great low price.

Debenhams. I would compare Debenhams stores in Britain to Kohl's, or J.C. Penney's stores in the United States.

My first experience in a Debenhams store was when searching for a swimsuit. I wanted to start taking scuba diving lessons, so I needed to get a swimsuit to participate in the required initial swimming pool sessions. At the time, I'd noticed a particularly striking swimsuit advertised at Debenhams on billboards all over town. Since I thought that this was perhaps the cutest bathing costume ever, I eventually made Brian take me shopping for the dreaded swimsuit, despite his many protests. They only had one left in my size, and it was perfect, so I nabbed it, together with a great floppy summer hat, and scooped both for a great price as well. Retail therapy at its best! Next, I have to begin the scuba lessons, so I can learn how to dive.

House of Fraser. In Manchester, this is one of my favourite department stores to browse around in. It has six floors in total, it's in the heart of the city I now live in. The stores have branches in most of the major cities in Britain, and they sell virtually everything you could possibly need. I would compare them to a Macy's store in the United States.

The House of Fraser stores are a bit pricier than other stores, such as Primark and even Debenhams, but they always sell the highest quality brands.

The store in Manchester used to be called Kendals, or Kendal Milne & Company, and this was where Brian first started working while he was still at high school. He maintained a part-time job in the book department there while working his way through studying at University. In those days, it was still considered to be one of the country's premier department stores, and I'd read about some of his adventures in his autobiography, "Tuxedo Warriors".

John Lewis. To date, I've only experienced the café at John Lewis, which was excellent. When we did so, we walked through the store rather quickly because we were meeting someone for tea, but from what I noticed, and Brian has confirmed this, John Lewis stores are upmarket, and similar to Nordstrom's stores in the United States.

Selfridges. This is another great higher-end store, and again, they are very similar to Nordstrom's stores in America. They have one at the Trafford Centre shopping mall in Manchester, and of course the "not to be missed"

211

flagship Selfridges store on Oxford Street in the centre of London. It's also well worth watching the great TV series about how the stores were founded, and some of their history. It's called "Mr Selfridge", and it's about the flamboyant Harry Gordon Selfridge who was an American-born retail tycoon that founded the world-famous British department stores of the same name.

Harvey Nichols. For some reason, I had never heard of this store before first arriving in Britain. I first became curious about them when my British girlfriends kept asking me, "Has Brian taken you to Harvey Nicks yet?" Initially, I didn't understand what all the fuss was about, however, all that was about to change.

The first time I went into a Harvey Nichols was with our other Anglo-American close friends, Suzy and Martin de Rooy. They are an amazing couple who have lived a balanced 50/50 lifestyle between Britain and the United States for almost 20 years. When we met there and wandered through the aisles, it was then when I understood why so many people had been asking me if I'd visited the store. This upmarket store is very much like a Bloomingdales in the United States.

You'll find all the main high-end designer brands there including, Valentino, Balmain, and Alexander McQueen etc. Harvey Nichols is a simply gorgeous store by any standards, and it's also a great place to while away an afternoon with girlfriends. It's a great place to visit for anyone who loves fashion and shopping, even if it's just window shopping.

The first time I visited a Harvey Nichols store, I didn't buy anything, and Suzy and Martin just showed me around before lunch. However, a few days later we were walking around the fabulous Manchester Christmas Markets with our friends Stuart and Sharon Hurst, and their daughter and son, Sophie and Oliver. (They are such a lovely family by the way, I just adore all of them!) Anyway, Sharon eventually led the way into Harvey Nichols.

While we were browsing, we noticed that they had special jars of Nutella for sale, and that you could have your

own name label printed and pasted on it. Of course, since I absolutely love all things chocolate, and especially Nutella, I fancied one with my own name on it and thought that after having lunch I'd go back and get one. However, before lunch had ended, Stuart had been exceptionally kind to me, and together with Oliver and Brian in collusion to serve as a distraction, he had slipped away to get me a gift of my very own jar of Nutella with "Helen" printed on it. I now use it to hold my spare change at home, and will never part with it. Perhaps it wasn't the most glamourous first thing to get from a Harvey Nicks store, but this lovely gift from the Hurst family is something that I will cherish forever.

Harrods. If you ever visit London, then you simply MUST visit Harrods in Knightsbridge. This is probably the premier store in the whole of Great Britain, and it's quite unlike anything I'd ever experienced before. It's fun to just walk around the store and admire the plethora of what can only be THE most luxurious and expensive brands in the world! This luxury high-end department store is unique, and we don't really have an equivalent in the United States. I suppose that the closest store that we have would be a Bloomingdales. However, I'm sorry Bloomingdales, you're good, really good in fact, but you're not even getting close to having the same opulence and magic of Harrods!

T.K. Maxx. Nope, that is not a misspelling in the name. In the United Kingdom T.J. Maxx is called T.K. Maxx. It's essentially exactly the same store, with the same deals, so go figure that one...

My first experience in a British T.K. Maxx – *and yes, it's still hard for me to both say, and write it that way* - was one in London's Covent Garden area. We were on our way to see my very first show in London, "The Woman in Black", so I naturally wanted to dress up a little for the occasion. I was wearing dress pants, a nice shirt, complimented by my high-heeled booties. Despite the heels height, the booties were always very comfortable, so I knew that I'd have no problem walking to the theatre in them while we soaked up the atmosphere of the Christmas light shows in the street, and shop window decorations.

Let me tell you that I now know for a fact, that British cobblestone streets and slightly worn heels on booties, do not mix well...

We'd left our hotel, which was just behind Leicester Square, and were walking casually through the Covent Garden area when I first felt the heel of my right bootie develop a slight wobble. At first, I just thought that it might be the cobblestone areas on the streets, but I was wrong. It was when I asked my husband Brian, to stop walking so that I could hold his shoulder for balance, while I lifted my foot to check out my heel. Unbelievably, and to my absolute horror, no sooner had my hand touched the heel of my bootie, that I felt it snap off completely! You can imagine how devastated I felt at the time, we were all dressed up, and on our way to have dinner before experiencing my first London theatrical show. By this time, if we would have gone back to the hotel to change, then we would have to miss dinner, and we'd almost certainly be late for the start of the show, which would have been terribly bad manners in itself.

So, drawing upon my Minnesotan/Alaskan pioneer spirit, I decided to "suck it up", I pulled up my proverbial "big girl panties" and decided to walk-on as if all was well. I'd simply deal with the aching leg muscles the next day.

I walked very gingerly and slowly, holding Brian's arm for support when needed, balancing my weight on the ball of my foot in my one good shoe. I remember thinking to myself, "Phew, that's not so bad. Hopefully nobody will notice that I'm sans one heel." It was after dinner when things took a turn for the worse. We'd resumed walking towards a point where we could catch a cab to the theatre to complete our journey. We'd just turned a street corner, when the one remaining good heel on my other bootie began to come lose and wobble! Furthermore, surprisingly for London, there wasn't a cab anywhere to be seen! It was then when I looked up and had never been more relieved to see a T.K. Maxx store, still open, and right in front of us. I glanced at Brian, and he returned my knowing glance, because we were both thinking the same thing.

At this point I didn't care what kind of shoes I would have to wear, I just wanted to be able to walk normally again and make it to the theatre on time. At the rate we were going, and unless we could find a cab that was empty, we were certainly going to be late. We went directly to the shoe aisle, and the first thing I see in my size, a black pair of Sketchers walking shoes. "Perfect!", I thought. So, we bought them right away. We were even more pleased when the cashier told us that they were on clearance, and therefore were only £11.00, or about $15.00! Even better! Once we'd bought the shoes and left the store, then lo and behold, there was an empty cab passing us every few moments! Go figure that one...

The show was awesome, meant in the true sense and meaning of the word, and we'd highly recommend it when you're in London. So much for me being uber-elegant and cool for my first London theatre experience. The very next day, Brian insisted that we visit a Russel and Bromley store on New Bond Street to buy an even more awesome pair of replacement booties.

Charity Shops. Charity shops in Britain are very much like the 2nd hand stores we have in the United States, and you can find some fabulous deals in them if you keep your eyes open.

217

For example, once we found a new Ted Baker brand baby pink leather biker jacket in a charity store, it had never been worn and the protective plastic film was still attached to the zips and metal fittings. The best part of all was that it only cost £40.00!

Whereas the very same jacket on sale in Harvey Nichols store cost close to £500.00! I know this, because I checked.

In another store, we even found an almost new Dolce and Gabbana brand coat for only £49.00, with the very same coat selling in Harvey Nichols for over £1,200.00! perhaps now you can see why I love the British charity stores so much.

Obviously, you can never tell what you'll find in them at any given time, but, this is what makes them so much fun. When you find a fantastic deal like either of these, it's a little like winning the lottery!

Boutiques. Boutiques of course are the same in Britain as they are in Minnesota. Sometimes they can be extremely overpriced, while at other times you can find a real bargain.

We were once shopping in the small town of Macclesfield, in Cheshire, when I was stopped in mid-step by a shop window display of small boutique. As soon as I

218

saw it, I immediately knew that this would be the perfect dress for our daughter's wedding. It was simply stunning,

and exactly what I had imagined, however, even before I went into the store, I was also pretty sure that it was going to be way out of my price range. I was completely wrong about that.

The owner of the store, Marion, told me that she was being forced to close her beloved shop because the council and landlords were hiking-up rents and local business taxes to beyond breaking point, so everything in the store was on sale-clearance. When she told me the price I was stunned, it was far less than I could have ever expected, so I immediately asked if I could try it on. It fit me perfectly, well, except for the length, because I'm only 4'11 ½" which is always an issue to be expected, so I bought it right away and will have it fitted. The lesson to be learned here, is that the answer is always NO, if you don't ask. You simply never know what bargains you'll find, and where you'll find them.

In Britain, there seem to be lots of bargains to be found if one only takes a little time to look around and search them out. Also. don't be put off if something initially appears to be out of your price range, because you simply never know for certain until you ask about it.

Now, we're all set for our daughter's big day, and I've got the perfect dress to wear for this very special occasion, and for others too. In case you were wondering, I sent her a picture of the dress before I bought it, and she loved it, so it had her seal of approval before the transaction was completed.

B&Q. B&Q in Britain is uncannily exactly the same as a Home Depot would be in the United States. It has exactly the same colours, layout and everything else. As an American walking into a B&Q store in Britain, you'd have to seriously second guess yourself that you'd not been beamed back to the United States without you noticing. The two stores are really that similar. You would also think that the two stores are brand-linked in some way, but surprisingly they are totally separate companies.

Shopping Snobbery. In Britain, there is a certain degree of snobbery attached to where you regularly shop for food. For example, shops like Aldi and Liddle are perceived to be at the bottom end of the shopping social scale, with Sainsbury's, Marks and Spencer, and Tesco would be in the mid, or upper mid-level. I'm not sure why some Brits are so snobby about this, so it remains a mystery and but being forewarned is forearmed.

Chapter 21: British Accents

If you ever tour Great Britain, then one of the first things that you'll notice is how very different the accents can be in different towns and regions, even if they're only a few miles apart geographically.

Naturally, I was well-aware that Scottish, Welsh or Northern Irish accents would be respectively different than other British accents. However, I was staggered to learn that there are about 56 different British accents in a country that is so small geographically. Furthermore, regardless of your monetary wealth, or lack of it, your accent will always define you.

Perhaps I shouldn't have been so surprised, because back in the United States, someone who is from Minnesota will have a very different accent than someone who is from Georgia, or one of the other Southern States. I suppose that in the back of my mind I tended to think that since Britain is so physically small in comparison to the United States, that there might be less variation per square mile instead of more.

Even in and around Manchester where we live, there are towns located less than 10 miles from the city centre, such as Salford, Bolton, and Oldham, and each have their own distinct accents. Also, the Liverpool accent is very different to that of the Manchester accent, even though the cities are only about 30 miles apart.

The reason why there are so many regional accents in such a small geographic area, goes back hundreds, if not, thousands of years. Back in those times making a journey of 10 miles or more, was a huge undertaking, so people tended to avoid it unless it was absolutely necessary. In addition to this, in those days the media didn't exist, which we now know tends to level-out accents and standardise vocabulary.

Many small pockets of distinctively different accents gradually built up over time. With the advent of the Industrial Revolution, it was suddenly possible for ordinary people to travel more easily over greater distances. When this happened, the micro-pockets of the numerous regional variations in accent tended to merge into larger regional variations. Eventually, this gave rise to the estimated 56 varieties of British accent that we have today.

Here are a few of the main variations in accents you will probably encounter when you're either visiting or living in the United Kingdom.

The Geordie Accent. This is roughly the accent of anyone from the upper North East England, especially around the Newcastle Upon Tyne area. A strong Geordie accent is typically representative of what the accent a working-class person would have from those areas. Some famous Geordies would be Rowan Atkinson, AKA Mr. Bean, Sting, AKA Gordon Sumner, and Hank Marvin.

The Welsh English Accent. Welsh-English is primarily spoken by the people in Wales and is directly influenced by the many nuances of the highly distinctive Welsh language. My husband, Brian, once took me to visit North Wales, which is absolutely beautiful, and while we were there we visited the town with the 2nd longest name in the world. I dare you to try and say it, aloud! It's called, "llanfairpwllgwyngyllgogerychwyrndrobwllllantysiliogogo-goch." I was particularly impressed to learn that Brian could actually say this name with quite a high degree of authenticity in his accent! He broke it down for me into block, how he had learned it, so that I might also try and learn how to say it, but so far, I've not had much luck. Here it is, and it might help you to say it too with practice. "Llan - Fair - Pwll - Gwyn - Gyll - Go - Ger - Ych - Wyrn - Drob - Wll - Llan - Ty - Silio - Go - Go – Goch." Some famous Welsh people are, Catherine Zeta-Jones, Richard Burton, and the singer, Tom Jones.

The Scottish English Accent. Obviously, this would be someone from Scotland, and a good example of a Scottish English accent would be that of Sean Connery, Ewan McGregor, or Gerard Butler. If you were to say, "I don't know" in a Scottish accent, then it might be pronounced something like, "I dinnae ken." "Ken" would mean to "know". Sometimes, accents can create misunderstandings, for example, the pronunciation of the word "pearl" in Scottish English could easily sound like the word "petal", which is completely unrelated to the original intended word. I know that this would be a problem for an American ear like my own because I've heard it said myself.

The Liverpool or "Scouse" Accent. "Scousers" are from Liverpool, which might also be referred to as Merseyside and the surrounding area. However, I'm also told that those from the surrounding area are lovingly known as "woollybacks" for some reason. The Liverpudlian

224

(someone from Liverpool) accent is very distinctive, and it sounds completely different to most other regional accents. Some famous "Scousers" are, The Beatles AKA Paul McCartney and John Lennon, also one of my personal favourites, Kim Cattrall.

The Cockney Accent. As you now know, the "Cockney" is now used to broadly describe all working-class people living in the City of London. It's highly distinctive, and they also developed their own special slang terms for many words. Instead of saying the word you wish to say itself, you would use two or three words in a phrase, with the last word rhyming with the original word you're referring to. It's a little complicated, and if you've not read that section yet because you've been skipping chapters in the book, then I'd advise you to read that chapter if you want to learn more about it. Some famous Cockneys, are Bob Hoskins, Helena Bonham Carter, David Beckham, and Michael Caine.

The Mancunian Accent. The Mancunian accent is the accent of someone from the City of Manchester. Naturally, this is now one of my favourites since my husband is from Manchester and we now live there. "Mancunian" is a term used for all people from Manchester, and not about people from any specific part or socio-economic class. This term was something new for me because I'd never heard it used before. A close friend of my husband Brian, Cliff Twemlow, is now a celebrated Mancunian whose picture has now been painted in huge murals around the city. Cliff wrote and recorded a now famous song called, "Mancunian Man" for the movies he wrote and produced called, "G.B.H." and "The Tuxedo Warrior". Other famous people from Manchester are, Sir Ian McKellan, and Peter Kay.

The West Country Accent. The West Country Accent would be heard around Cornwall, Dorset, Devon and the West Country area in general. Cornwall is one of our favourite places to visit, and I especially love the accent of the people in that area. Roger Taylor, the drummer from the legendary band, Queen, and Mick Fleetwood, of Fleetwood Mac are from that part of the world. Some amazing TV shows have also been filmed in Cornwall, including, "Poldark", "Doc Martin", and "Jamaica Inn".

The Yorkshire Accent. The Yorkshire dialect is spoken typically in Northern England, and especially in the county of Yorkshire. People with a Yorkshire accent would tend to clip their words and contract them when said.

For example, "Yes, I'll have a drink." When said by a person with a broad Yorkshire accent would be something like, "Aye, I'll 'ave a drink." Another example would be when someone needs a toilet, and in a standard English accent would say, "I need the toilet." which would translate in a Yorkshire accent to, "I need't loo." Since I love shopping, if were to say, "I love the shopping mall." then it would translate to something like, "I love-tuh mall." They'd completely drop the word "shopping" from the sentence.

Some famous people from Yorkshire are, Ed Sheeran, Dame Judi Dench, and Sir Patrick Stewart. This is also the accent that I'm used to hearing in the British TV show I particularly love, Heartbeat.

PBS TV and BBC TV. I'd highly recommend that anyone from America wishing to explore more of the regional accents of Britain, to do so by watching the PBS TV channel in the United States. The PBS channel broadcasts many of the excellent British TV shows, most of which are from the BBC, which contain a great many of the U.K.'s regional accents including, "Poldark", "Doc Martin", "Downton Abbey", and many more.

If for some reason you're intrigued to learn more about the Manchester accent, and that of the surrounding areas, then you can also do this through your TV set. I'd highly recommend watching the BBC time travel series "Life on Mars" and the follow-on series, "Ashes to Ashes". They are both amazing shows with an incredibly fascinating storyline, and you'll get to hear some of Manchester's finest accents portrayed by the talented actors.

Losing Your Accent for Another. Since I moved to Britain, many of my friends and family have jokingly said that I might one day lose my accent, and sound more like a Brit. I've got some bad news for them because it's highly unlikely to happen. This is because scientists suggest the phenomenon of losing your native accent to adopt another by first adopting the local vocabulary. Then later, assuming a foreign accent as an adult, is borne either out of empathy, or more likely, a subconscious desire to fit in. The latter isn't me. I love my new home, I have empathy for, and love the people here, and I also love their accent, but I'll fit in best by just being Minnesotan "me" and not by becoming someone else.

Chapter 22: Royalty and Conclusion

In the United States we obviously don't have a Royal Family, so, we're left with whichever politician has become President of the United States, and then a string of Hollywood and media

celebrities instead.   Even though many of them are fabulous people, they still all fall way short in comparison to genuine Royalty.

I've always loved the Royal Family in Great Britain.

Her Majesty Queen Elizabeth II
Photo by Joel Rouse, Ministry of Defence
www.defenceimagery.mod.uk
Wikipedia

Curiously, Her Majesty The Queen and my husband Brian's Mother both bear an uncanny strikingly similarity to each other in how they look.

I also clearly remember as a young girl, watching on TV when Princess Diana was married to Prince Charles, and how it all looked exactly like a real fairy-tale wedding. I just adored Princess

Diana, and avidly followed her exploits and travels throughout her short life. Also, like a great many others, I was completely devastated to learn of her untimely death.

**The British Royal Family
on the balcony of Buckingham Palace**
Photo by Carfax2 – Wikipedia

Over the years since that time, it has been a great joy for me to watch both Prince William, and Prince Harry, grow up to become fine men. I enjoyed every moment of watching Prince William get married to his fabulous, elegant and gorgeous wife, The Duchess of Cambridge, Kate Middleton. I feel in my heart that they are such a happy family, and that they're setting a great example of how to be both a loving couple, and good parents. Perhaps these are important lessons that everyone can learn from in some way. To me at least, and it may sound corny, but, I'm completely sincere in what I say. I believe that they are exemplary role models in a world where we have so precious few of them these days.

More recently, I was simply overjoyed to learn about Prince Harry becoming engaged to the beautiful Meghan Markle. They look perfect together as a couple, and I'd been a huge fan of Meghan's from the very first time

I saw her in the TV show "Suits". From the outside, looking in at least, I think that they will complement each other perfectly in a great many ways. Since Meghan was already heavily involved in volunteer charity work before she met Prince Harry, and since the Royal Family have always been heavily involved in similar work, then I'm certain that she will be a perfect fit into an already fabulous family.

My husband and I are both very excited for them, and for their future together as a couple. Also, perhaps unsurprisingly, we love that Prince Harry is marrying an ordinary American girl, just like I am. Perhaps this is why I, and millions of others in America, as well as people all over the world, can relate to them both so easily. I believe that this marriage also marks the beginning of a new and even brighter future for the Royal Family. Over the past few decades they have been able to gradually change their public persona and image marvellously, and in effect, reinvent themselves for the 21st century. This is terrific to see, and a joy to behold.

As a girl, I never even dreamed that I would ever meet my very own British gentleman, let alone that one day I'd be married to him and I would be living in England. My own husband might not be a real Prince, but, to me he is MY very own Prince Charming, and I am truly blessed beyond belief.

Since I married my British gentleman, we've both been on a wonderful life-journey together which has been filled with love, joy, happiness and laughter at every twist and turn. Most of which has originated from the fact that we're from two different countries that share a common culture, and a common language, that's just sufficiently different enough to still cause lots of belly-laughs along the way. Therefore, we know that this book will be especially useful for every Anglo-American couple, and especially for who are newlyweds. The Royal newlyweds included.

We began to wonder how often Prince Harry and Meghan Markle have experienced many of the same unavoidable situations, and hilarious conversations about our Anglo-American differences that my husband and I have shared together. At times, it seems that our common

Meghan Markle and Prince Harry
Photo by Mark Jones - Wikipedia

language and culture can be a barrier in itself. This is how the idea behind this this book came about.

In addition, it was conceived through our genuine love of the Royal Family. When Prince Harry and Meghan Markle got engaged, the first thing I said to my husband upon hearing the news was, "I bet that they will experience many of the same transatlantic differences and conversations we have, especially since she'll be moving to England now that she's joining the Royal Family."

Before long, I was writing this book and having a wonderful time researching all the anecdotes, idioms, alternative meanings, and other items of interest written into it. It's been a great departure from writing our more usual books about fitness and exercise etc., and it's been a very enjoyable diversion. I've loved every minute of exploring our commonalities, and our difference, and especially how and why they first occurred.

Furthermore, I can honestly say, that being an American married to a Brit, is a joyous adventure for us both in so many ways, each and every day.

My husband and I both proudly dedicate this book to Prince Harry and Meghan Markle, on the occasion of their wedding, 19th May 2018.

We wish them both, good health, long life, and happiness in every way! Also, as an Anglo-American couple, just like we are, we already know that this book will be very useful to them both on a great many occasions as they settle down to their future life together!

www.MajorVision.com

The 70 Second Difference™

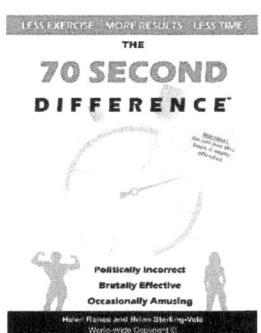

Stop confusing activity with accomplishment by exercising the traditional way with long exercise sessions, and with less than scientific guesses about how much and how many you need to do, of sets and repetitions.

Your time is too precious to waste, and time is the number 1 reason why people either stop exercising regularly, or don't exercise to begin with.

Big fitness club chains and gyms, want to make you believe that it takes hours of time each week, and that all their expensive and bulky equipment is essential for you to get a complete workout. You don't need all of this, and you certainly don't need to spend hours and hours of time each week just to exercise.

Just 70 seconds of focussed ISOfitness™ exercise daily has been scientifically proven to make you stronger, fitter, more muscular, and reduce your body fat. It will give you more results, with less exercise, and in less time than any other system because it's the appliance of science, NOT guesswork.

To many, The 70 Second Difference™ approach is controversial. However, this is almost certainly because we're openly focused only on proven science-based results, science-based exercise, and scientific data about nutrition. We also explain the science and the inconvenient truths about many popular food sources, why bodybuilders and strength athletes are so physically different, how much protein you really need, weight control and weight loss, as well as the real science behind muscle growth and strength.

The 70 Second Difference™ approach to exercise utilises special short burst, highly focussed isometric exercises which are proven to be superior to old fashioned traditional exercise methods in over 5,500 independent scientific studies.

The 70 Second Difference™ explains how ISOfitness™ exercise engages your natural Adaptive Response™ mechanism, which means that everyone benefits from the same exercises in roughly equal percentages of improvement. This means that both unfit beginners and top professional athletes will all get the perfect workout that's right for them at their individual level of strength and fitness.

The 70 Second Difference™ is also a special workout routine using ISOfitness™ exercises. It is designed to give you a highly effective full-body workout in only 70 seconds of continuous exercise time.

Required Equipment: 2 x Iso-Bows® - available on Amazon.com, or direct from Bullworker.com

The ISO90™ Course

ISO90™ is a comprehensive and complete step by step 90-day/12-week body shaping, bodybuilding and functional strength building course based on the ISOfitness™ system of isometric exercises.

Since the ISO90™ course engages your body's natural Adaptive Response™ mechanism, it is ideal for beginners, advanced athletes, and even for professional-level athletes. This is because at whatever level you're at the more intensity you apply to each exercise, the faster and more efficiently your body will respond.

The ISO90™ course focusses the appliance of science in practical exercise and functional strength building, and in doing so, it makes the ISO90™ 90-day/12-week course, one of the fastest, and most efficient ways to get into shape, build muscle, and get strong which has ever been devised.

The ISO90™ course is also designed with time, ease of use, and flexibility in mind. This means that you benefit from a professional-level workout literally anywhere, and on almost any location.

Each week will build upon the gains and improvements made in previous weeks, with clear instruction and pictures to demonstrate how each exercise should be performed.

The ISO90™ course can be used as a stand-alone body shaping, bodybuilding, and functional strength building course.

Required Equipment: 2 x Iso-Bows - available on Amazon.com

Workout at Work™

A stark new warning from the Icahn School of Medicine at Mount Sinai School of Medicine in New York reveals that sitting at a desk working for more than 6 hours a day can be extremely damaging to your health, and even exercising 4 evenings a week after work, or for long periods over the weekend, won't fix the damage.

The average person spends over 10 years of their life at work over an average 45 year working life, which for most people means sitting at a desk for a staggering 10-years of their life! Time, or lack of it, is also working against after-work exercise sessions. Exercising the traditional way in a gym 3-days a week, will consume a further 4.27 years. Therefore, time is the #1 reason why people don't exercise.

The fact is that sitting at a desk for more than 6 hours a day can cause potentially irreversible damage can be done to your heart, together with increases in both cholesterol and body fat, as well as insulin resistance which is a precursor to type 2 diabetes.

What if you could workout effectively while you were at work? What if a complete beginner could exercise with equal ease to someone who is an advanced athlete, and all without leaving your place of work?

Now you can do exactly that with The ISOfitness™ system of advanced isometric exercises. With the ISOfitness™ system, and a pair of Iso-Bows®, the world's smallest total-body exerciser, you can workout effectively at work, no matter what fitness level you're at, without ever leaving your desk!

Even if you perform just one 7-second high-intensity exercise every 30 minutes, you'll gain maximum benefit from this scientifically proven system. At the end of a 9-hour working day you can easily perform an 18-20 exercise total-body workout, so you leave work healthier, fitter stronger, and with more time to spend with family and friends.

Your boss won't complain either, because in exchange for just 126 seconds out of your working day, you'll be up to 30% more efficient at your job, and you'll take less time off sick.

Required Equipment: 2 x Iso-Bows - available on Amazon.com

Fitness on the Move™

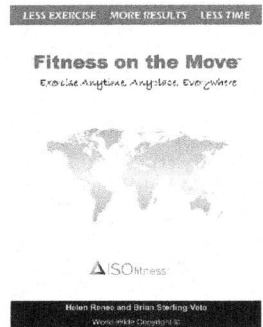

Time is the #1 reason why people don't exercise. The #2 reason is lack of access to a gym.

With the ISOfitness™ system of Fitness on the Move™ There are no more excuses. You can literally workout anytime, anyplace, everywhere, thanks to the ISOfitness™ exercise system of advanced isomeric exercises, combined with the powerful Iso-Bow®.

The advanced isometric exercises of the ISOfitness™ system have been scientifically proven in thousands of independent experiments to be superior to traditional exercise methods.

We've tried and tested the Fitness on the Move™ system by performing full workout routines as passengers in cars, on trains, in cramped airline seats, on mountainsides, on beaches, and once even on the deck of a ship in a storm.

The ISOfitness™ system of Fitness on the Move™ allows a full-body workout in the smallest space humanly possible thanks to our Zero Footprint Workout™ concept. With the Fitness on the Move™ system you never need to miss a workout ever again.

Required Equipment: 2 x Iso-Bows - available on Amazon.com

The SSASS™ Course

The Sixty Second ASS Workout™, or SSASS™ workout, is the fastest and most effective ass workout ever devised.

Based on the scientifically proven principles of the ISOfitness™ exercise system, the SSASS™ workout is a no-nonsense, no time-wasting workout that really does do everything you need to make your ass, tight, firm, shapely, and strong.

TIME, and more precisely the lack of it, is the #1 reason why people either don't exercise, or stop exercising. Life and work can just get in the way of exercise plans, and before you know it, it's been weeks since you had a workout.

The SSASS™ routine means no more time-wasting workouts where you twist, shake, waggle your ass, kick your legs, or dance around for 30 minutes. None of which really target the area you want. Time is short, and it's your choice if you want to waste it by waggling your ass to music because it "feels" good, or, if you want to get the job done in just 60 seconds of laser-focussed ISOfitness™ exercse.

Everyone has 60 seconds of time to spare, even on the busiest day, so, you're Just 60 seconds a day from having a great ass.

Required Equipment: 2 x Iso-Bows - available on Amazon.com

The Bullworker Bible™

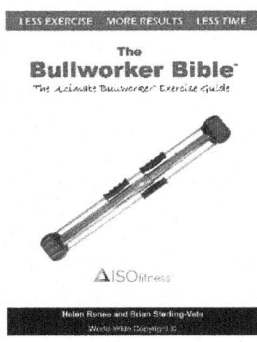

The Bullworker Bible™ is the definitive resource guide for all Bullworker® users, and it's the companion book for The Bullworker 90™ Course.

The Bullworker Bible™ is approved by the makers, and distributors of The Bullworker, at Bullworker.com

The Bullworker Bible™ is the complete science-based user-friendly guide of how the Bullworker should be used properly to deliver maximum results. It also shows you how to effectively use the Bow Extension® and the Steel Bow®.

It gives you all the information that you always wanted to know, but the simple wall charts, and very basic instruction manuals didn't.

⚠ How Repetition-Compression Speed Control is Essential
⚠ Correct Breathing Techniques
⚠ Hooke's Law of Physics and The Bullworker™
⚠ Correct Biomechanics for Best Results

The Bullworker Bible™ is also the essential guide for all users of the Bullworker X5, Bully Extreme, ISO 7x, and the Bullworker X7.

Brian Sterling-Vete is an internationally acclaimed exercise scientist and martial arts lifetime achievement award-winner who is also a 45+ year Bullworker® user. He used the Bullworker® to coach his friend and 4 times World's Strongest Man, Jon Pall Sigmarsson of Iceland.

Required Equipment: A Bullworker® Classic, or a similar device.

Recommended Additional Equipment: Steel Bow®, Bow Extension® kit, 2 x Iso-Bows®.

The Bullworker 90™ Course

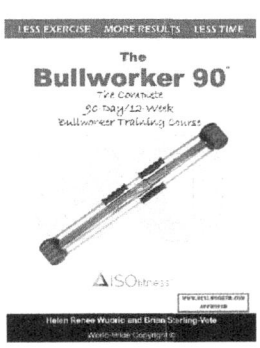

The Bullworker 90™ Course is the essential 90-day/12-week course for all Bullworker® users, and it's the companion book to The Bullworker Bible™

The Bullworker 90™ Course is approved by the makers, and distributors of The Bullworker, at Bullworker.com

The Bullworker 90™ is a 400+ page, science-based, user-friendly, step-by-step course designed to increase strength, fitness, grow muscle, body-build, and increase power over a 90-day/12-week period.

The Bullworker 90™ Course is a detailed exercise plan which progressively increases in intensity, as the days and weeks progress. New exercises are added almost every week, with complete routine changes every two weeks.

Each week has a detailed note section, together with suggestions about exercise days, and rest times etc., so that you know exactly what to do, and when to do it.

- ⚠ Step-by-step, week-by-week instruction
- ⚠ Progressively increasing intensity over 90 days
- ⚠ Routine changes every two weeks
- ⚠ Isotonic and Isometric exercise combinations
- ⚠ Multi-angle isometric exercise combinations

The Bullworker 90™ Course is designed by the authors of The Bullworker Bible™, and can be used with the Bullworker® Classic, the Steel Bow®, the Bullworker X5, the Bully Extreme, the ISO 7x, and the Bullworker X7.

The Bullworker 90™ Course also contains alternative/extra exercises which incorporate the use of the Iso-Bow®, and the Bow Extension®, that can be used with all Bullworker-type exercisers to increase the range and effectiveness of the device.

Required Equipment: A Bullworker® Classic, or a similar device. Recommended Additional Equipment: Steel Bow®, Bow Extension® kit, 2 x Iso-Bows®.

Mental Martial Arts

MENTAL
MARTIAL ARTS
THE SHAOLIN SECRETS
FOR BUSINESS... AND LIFE

BRIAN STERLING-VETE

Brian Sterling-Vete's Mental Martial Arts is a system of intellectual life-combat skills which uses the tactics and principles of the physical martial arts. All interaction in life, at your place of work, in your business, and when negotiating and communicating with others, is an exchange of energy, power and influence. During these interactions, one party is always exerting maximum influence over the other as they attempt

243

to gain the outcome they prefer over the weaker party. The more powerful and persuasive will usually end as the winner. A physical analogy would be that of a bigger, stronger, and more powerful person gaining influence over a smaller, weaker person by bullying, intimidating, and even by physical violence. This is unless the apparently "weaker" person is trained in the martial arts...

Using Brian's unique system of Mental Martial Arts, you can learn to verbally, intellectually, and emotionally guide, channel, and redirect the energy of others, even more powerful people and large organisations. In doing so, you achieve the outcome you desire in both life and business. Brian's Mental Martial Arts system contains a specific section to help those who may be forced to face a potentially hostile media in the event of a crisis. In this section, Brian combines his system of Mental Martial Arts, together with the experience he gained in over a decade with BBC TV News, to help you and your organisation stay "Media Safe". www.mentalmartialarts.tv

Tuxedo Warriors

Tuxedo Warriors is the companion book to The Tuxedo Warrior. This is the autobiography of author, composer, movie-maker Cliff Twemlow. The book ended at the beginning of what has been called the Golden Age of Video Cinematography, which he inspired.

The new book, Tuxedo Warriors is the most complete biography of Cliff Twemlow ever written. It's also the autobiography Brian Sterling-Vete, who played a central role in this unique, entertaining, and true story of two extraordinary "Renaissance-Men", and their adventures as guerrilla movie-makers.

Brian and Cliff traversed the globe on many previously untold adventures in Iceland, and the Arctic Circle, in the Mediterranean, in North Africa and a war zone, on tramp-steamer journeys across the ocean, and on road trips across continents.

Tuxedo Warriors is told by Brian Sterling-Vete, and he continues the story where the original book ends. Brian is perhaps the only person who can tell the complete story from the time it all began, right through until the end, with sudden and untimely death of his great friend Cliff.

Cliff and his works have now become known globally, even achieving "cult" status, primarily thanks to great work of Dr Chris Lee and Andy Wills in their excellent book "The Lost World of CLIFF TWEMLOW: The King of Manchester Exploitation Movies", re-releases of his movies, and through TV documentaries.

Tuxedo Warriors is a compelling, entertaining, and true story about two extraordinary characters who were pioneers during this pivotal and innovative period in the history of world cinema. Tuxedo Warriors is the sequel to the book, and movie by Cliff Twemlow: "The Tuxedo Warrior", Starring: John Wyman, Carol Royle, Holly Palance, John Terry and James Coburn Jnr.

The Tuxedo Warrior by Cliff Twemlow – Prologue and epilogue by Brian Sterling-Vete

There are many ways in which a Doorman can gain respect. Numerous methods applied to the principal. In my profession, every available technique must be utilised, depending on the situation and circumstances.

Would-be transgressors either move-off the premises quietly acknowledging your diplomatic approach. Or, the other alternative whereby physical persuasion must be exercised, which either quells their pugilistic desires, or it triggers their aggressive instincts, turning the whole incident into a bloody and violent encounter.

'The Tuxedo Warrior,' pulls no punches in its brawling, savage, colourful, and entertaining exposure of society's nightlife activities.

The above, is the original text from the rear cover of Cliff's book. Cliff and I were extremly close friends, and I'm honoured to re-publish his original work, which completes the storyline of my own book, 'Tuxedo Warriors.'

Where Cliff's original book ends, my own book overlaps and begins, to complete his colourful life story. I'm also honoured to be close friends with his eldest son, Barry Twemlow, and sincerely thank him for writing a foreword to make this re-published book even more complete.

246

The Pike by Cliff Twemlow – Prologue and epilogue by Brian Sterling-Vete

ITS FIRST VICTIMS

A screeching swan... A fisherman overboard... A drunken woman...

One by one, the mysterious killer in Lake Windermere claims its terrified victims. Tearing off limbs with its monstrous teeth, horribly mutilating bodies. Fear sweeps the peaceful holiday resort when experts identify the creature as a giant pike.... A hellish creature with the strength to rupture boats, and the anger to attack them.

But for some, the terror becomes a bonanza—the traders who cater to the gathering crowds of ghouls on the shore. And, they will do anything to stop divers finding the creature. Meanwhile the ripples of bloodshed widen....
The Pike

The above, is the original text from the rear cover of Cliff's book. I remember this book going into pre-production as a major movie in the early 1980's starring Joan Collins. Sadly, the financiers ran into personal difficulties and it was never made.

Today, there is now renewed interest in this book as a screenplay and movie. In my own book, 'Tuxedo Warriors,' I tell the behind the scenes story of myself, my close friend Cliff Twemlow, and The Pike.

The Beast of Kane by Cliff Twemlow – Prologue and epilogue by Brian Sterling-Vete

When the Gordon Family open their door to a stray Elkhound, they unwittingly welcome-in the forces of evil. For, according to the local priest, the huge dog is Satan himself, fulfilling an ancient prophecy.

But, no one will believe this warning... Even when sheep – and wolves – are mysteriously slaughtered. Even when frenzied pets turn on their owners. Even when Emily Forrest is savagely eaten alive – the first of many human victims.

As winter tightens its icy grip on the remote town of Kane, its unprotected people must face an unearthly terror.

The above, is the original text from the rear cover of Cliff's book. This was the first of Cliff's books to be accepted by Hammer Film Studios to be made into a big-screen horror movie, along with Cliff's other book, The Pike.

More importantly, the reason why it was never to be made into a movie was no reflection on the book itself. It was entirely because of the increasing financial challenges Hammer Films were facing at that time. They were issues that were so serious, that they caused the unexpected and rapid decline of the studio.

www.MajorVision.com

Made in the USA
Columbia, SC
12 April 2018